THE ESSENTIAL GUIDE TO SUICIDE PREVENTION

Transformative Strategies for Reducing Self-Harm, Enhancing Mental Health and Building Personal Resilience

---

VERNON MULLINS, MSN, APRN, FNP-BC

© Copyright Vernon T. Mullins
Resilient Minds Publishing, LLC
(2024) - All rights reserved.

The content within this book may not be reproduced, duplicated, or transmitted without direct written permission from the author or the publisher.

Under no circumstances will any blame or legal responsibility be held against the publisher or author for any damages, reparation, or monetary loss due to the information contained within this book, either directly or indirectly. You are responsible for your own choices, actions, and results.

Legal Notice:

This book is copyright protected. This book is only for personal use. You cannot amend, distribute, sell, use, quote, or paraphrase any part of the content within this book without the consent of the author or publisher.

Disclaimer Notice:

Please note the information contained within this document is for educational and entertainment purposes only. All effort has been expended to present accurate, up-to-date, reliable, and complete information. No warranties of any kind are declared or implied. Readers acknowledge that the author is not engaging in the rendering of legal, financial, medical, or professional advice. The content within this book has been derived from various sources. Please consult a licensed professional before attempting any techniques outlined in this book.

By reading this document, the reader agrees that under no circumstances is the author responsible for any losses, direct or indirect, which are incurred as a result of the use of the information contained within this document, including, but not limited to, errors, omissions, or inaccuracies.

Dedication

This book is dedicated to families worldwide who have felt the deep and lasting impact of suicide, who have lost cherished loved ones to this tragic epidemic. It is for those who pour their hearts and souls into helping others recognize the true value of their lives, to see their worth and meaning within this beautiful existence. To those striving to make a difference, I offer this work with hope and compassion.

To all who have experienced loss or endured hardship or who are currently struggling themselves may this book be a beacon of hope, illuminating paths once shadowed by darkness. For those seeking to support others, I hope it provides the resources, tools, and insights you need on your journey to lift up those you love.

Love one another, sacrifice for one another, and do not hesitate to help others discover the beauty within themselves. By sharing in each other's burdens, we can rise above the challenges that weigh us down. Let's embrace the joy in helping others make the most of this beautiful life by guiding them to love themselves.

With hope & sincerity,
Vernon Mullins, MSN, APRN, FNP-BC

Table of Contents

Introduction	9
1. THE MANY FACES OF SUICIDAL IDEATION	13
1.1 The Spectrum of Suicidal Thoughts: From Passive to Active	14
1.2 Recognizing Signs in Loved Ones: Beyond the Words	16
1.3 The Role of Mental Illness in Suicidal Ideation	19
1.4 Debunking Myths: What Suicidal Ideation Does and Doesn't Mean	22
1.5 The Impact of Social Media: A Double-Edged Sword	24
1.6 Cultural Influences on Perceptions of Suicide	28
1.7 Navigating Suicidal Ideation in LGBTQ+ Communities	31
1.8 Veterans and Suicidal Thoughts: A Closer Look at PTSD	34
1.9 Suicidal Ideation in Adolescents: Understanding the Teenage Mind	38
1.10 Addressing Suicidal Ideation in the Elderly: Loneliness and Beyond	42
2. CULTIVATING MINDFULNESS AND EMOTIONAL RESILIENCE	45
2.1 Grounding in the Present	46
2.2 The Power of Positive Thinking: Reshaping Your Narrative	49
2.3 Emotional Regulation in Times of Crisis	52
2.4 The Importance of Self-Compassion on the Road to Resilience	56
2.5 Setting Boundaries for Mental Health	59
2.6 The Role of Physical Health in Building Resilience	63
2.7 Finding Purpose After Loss	66

2.8 Nurturing Hope: The Seed of Resilience 69
2.9 Creative Expression as a Pathway Out of Darkness 72

3. FORGING CONNECTIONS FOR HEALING 77
3.1 Identifying and Accessing Support Systems 78
3.2 The Importance of Peer Support Groups in Healing 81
3.3 Role of Family Dynamics in Suicide Prevention 84
3.4 How to Offer Support Without Offering Solutions 88
3.5 Creating Safe Spaces for Open Conversations 91
3.6 The Power of Community Programs in Suicide Prevention 94
3.7 Technology and Apps: Modern Tools for Connection 97
3.8 Educators as Pillars of Support: A Guide for Schools 101
3.9 Workplace Mental Health: Building a Supportive Culture 104
3.10 Spiritual Communities: A Resource for Hope and Healing 107

4. NAVIGATING THROUGH GRIEF AND HEALING 111
4.1 Understanding the Grieving Process: A Guide for the Bereaved 112
4.2 Trauma-Informed Care: Principles and Practices 115
4.3 The Role of Therapy: Finding the Right Fit 118
4.4 Navigating the Complexities of Survivor's Guilt 122
4.5 Healing Rituals and Remembrance: Honoring Loved Ones 125
4.6 Journaling as a Tool for Healing 128
4.7 The Impact of Community Memorials and Vigils 131
4.8 The Healing Power of Nature: Ecotherapy Insights 134
4.9 Art Therapy: Expressing the Inexpressible 136
4.10 Moving Forward: Rebuilding Life After Loss 138

5. EMPOWERING CHANGE: SUICIDE PREVENTION IN ACTION 141
5.1 Suicide Prevention Training: Empowering First Responders 142
5.2 The Role of Media in Shaping Suicide Awareness 144

5.3 Implementing School-Based Suicide Prevention Programs	147
5.4 Holistic Approaches to Mental Health: Beyond Traditional Therapy	155
5.5 Advocacy and Policy Change: A Path to Systemic Support	158
5.6 How to Start a Conversation About Suicide Prevention	162
5.7 Creating a Suicide Prevention Plan: A Guide for Families	165
5.8 The Importance of Crisis Hotlines: A Lifeline for Many	168
5.9 Reducing Access to Means: A Preventative Strategy	171
5.10 The Future of Suicide Prevention: Trends and Innovations	173
Conclusion	179
Quick Access Reference List for Suicide Prevention and Awareness	183
References	187

Introduction

At the heart of what makes us human, amid the decadent and unique diversity of our experiences, there's a simple, beautiful truth that ties us all together: the fact that we are all even here. We are alive! This shared journey of existence, this precious gift of life, unites us all. We find our connection through shared experiences of struggle and resilience, whether in quiet moments or milestones, happiness or heartache. The idea that just one life can change the course of history is truly remarkable, a vivid reminder of the incredible potential and value each of us carries within, encouraging us to evolve and thrive amidst life's perpetual flux, pushing us past who we were yesterday. As we reflect on life's immense beauty and potential, it becomes beyond heartbreaking to realize that for some, this beauty fades into the shadows of their struggles, making the prospect of moving forward feel insurmountable.

Our individual journeys through life mirror our uniqueness, each threaded with its blend of joy, sorrow, and obstacles, as varied and distinct as we are. Acknowledging the distinctiveness of our paths is crucial as we each navigate through life marked by personal challenges that are uniquely our own. The pull towards thoughts of ending one's life is a dark chapter of the human experience, challenging to navigate yet absolutely crucial to confront.

This book aims to tackle the topic of suicide with an open heart, bringing to light thoughts and feelings that are often left unspoken out of fear or discomfort surrounding this heavy topic. The importance of suicide prevention and awareness can't be understated. Through honest daily conversations and actionable insights, I hope this book resonates with people from all walks of life, wherever they may be, touching the hearts of those who are silently struggling and serving as a tool for those seeking to help them. As we approach this sensitive subject, it's essential to acknowledge that specific discussions within these pages may resonate deeply, potentially triggering discomfort or distress, particularly for those touched by suicide or experiencing thoughts of self-harm. My foremost hope and intention is to foster a space for open, heartfelt conversation and share practical insights to support those in need.

My personal experience with the profound impact of suicide began with the loss of a high school friend. His vibrant smile and outgoing nature hid a world of inner turmoil I only came to understand after his passing. His internal battle with feelings of self-worth, complicated by personal and family issues, hidden battles with substance use, and troubled relationships, revealed the intricate and often silent struggle with suicidality that many endure, mirroring his own. Since his passing, hardly a year has gone by without feeling the impact of suicide within my personal and professional worlds. Some years more acutely than others. In the last two years, coinciding with the period this book took shape, five individuals from my circles have been tragically lost to suicide. The weight of this reality hits me deeply. In the United

States alone, as reported by the CDC in 2023, suicide remains a leading cause of death, with nearly 50,000 lives lost in 2022 alone, marking a slight increase from the year before. With nearly twenty years of experience in the medical field amidst the rapid pace of the emergency room, the intensities of inpatient care, and the diverse challenges of outpatient services, I've encountered numerous individuals grappling with thoughts of suicide. A crucial observation I've obtained from these interactions is the significant impact that a sense of connection and belongingness has in countering the deep-seated loneliness associated with suicidal ideation. These feelings, often experienced during struggles with suicidal ideation, underscore the profound importance of connection and belonging. Their absence can profoundly erode an individual's sense of self-worth and intrinsic value, diminishing the motivation to continue living. This lack can lead to self-destructive thoughts, depression, and anxiety, further isolating individuals from the support they crucially need.

To truly address suicidality, we must strengthen the bonds of human connection, underscoring the importance of love, understanding, and belonging in living full, meaningful lives. It's about reinforcing these connections that can help reduce and even prevent suicide worldwide. This book is my attempt at an honest, heartfelt conversation about the complexities of suicidality, offering insights and suggestions for individuals and communities alike. While I don't claim to be a mental health expert, my experiences—personal and professional—have bestowed me with a compassionate outlook that I hope will contribute meaningfully to this crucial dialogue.

This book is more than just words on a page—it's a heartfelt invitation for all of us to show compassion, to listen genuinely, and to support one another. By doing so, we don't just confront the issue of suicide; we affirm every individual's inherent worth and potential. Through these pages, I hope to empower each reader with the tools and courage to build resilience, fully embrace life, and unlock our collective and individual potential to the fullest. Let's join hands in overcoming the shadows that seek to drag us down, triumph over adversity in life's moments of darkness, and march towards a future bright with strength, resilience, and the promise of survival. Together, let's journey beyond suicide towards a horizon of renewed hope and light.

ONE

The Many Faces of Suicidal Ideation

In the quiet moments of reflection, when our thoughts meander through the bright and dark corners of our minds, there exists a spectrum that isn't often talked about openly, yet so many of us navigate it silently. Suicidal thoughts, a topic clouded in misconceptions and apprehension, encompass a wide range—from fleeting desires for escape to detailed thoughts of self-harm. This chapter is here to unravel this spectrum, providing a more in-depth understanding of its nuances and stressing the importance of identifying its indicators at each phase.

1.1 The Spectrum of Suicidal Thoughts: From Passive to Active

Suicidal ideation, a term that encompasses thoughts about or an unusual preoccupation with suicide, varies significantly in intensity and intention. Understanding this continuum is crucial, as it aids in providing appropriate support and intervention.

Understanding the Continuum

At one end of the spectrum lie passive suicidal thoughts. These thoughts may manifest as wishes to go to sleep and not wake up or desires for an end to pain without a deliberate intention to act on these wishes. Contrary to active suicidal ideation, where there is a detailed plan and a desire to carry it out, passive ideation lacks a concrete plan for suicide. Understanding this distinction is vital for both individuals experiencing these thoughts and those supporting them, as it guides the approach to intervention.

Identifying Risk Levels

Identifying the seriousness of suicidal ideation involves keen observation and open communication. Signs to watch for include changes in behavior, such as withdrawal from social interactions, alterations in mood, or expressions of hopelessness. Verbal cues, although sometimes subtle, can provide critical insights. Statements like "I'm tired of everything" or "I wish I could disappear" may indicate passive ideation, whereas more direct expressions such as "I've thought about how I would do it" suggest active ideation. Recognizing these signs and their implications is the first step toward providing effective and practical support.

The Importance of Early Intervention

Early recognition and timely intervention can drastically change the trajectory of someone experiencing suicidal thoughts. It's a common misconception that talking about suicide can plant the idea in someone's mind. Open dialogue can provide relief and serve as a bridge to seeking professional help. Ensuring early intervention by understanding where an individual falls on the spectrum of suicidal ideation guarantees that tailored support and resources are provided, potentially averting a crisis.

For instance, when a teacher notices a student's persistent disengagement and expressions of self-doubt, addressing these observations directly with the student can open a pathway to support further. It's about creating an environment where the individual feels seen and heard, validating their feelings while offering hope and resources.

Misconceptions About Passive Ideation

People often misunderstand and sometimes dismiss passive suicidal thoughts as non-serious or not warranting attention. This misconception can lead to missed opportunities for connection and support. It's critical to understand that any form of suicidal ideation is a signal of deep psychological pain and deserves compassionate attention. Acknowledging and addressing passive ideation can be preventive, offering individuals the support they need before thoughts escalate to active planning.

For example, consider someone who confides in a friend about feeling overwhelmed and wishing they could disappear. This expression of passive ideation invites empathy, understanding, and support, not dismissal. It's a moment to offer a listening ear, validate their feelings, and gently guide them toward professional help.

In navigating the spectrum of suicidal thoughts, understanding and empathy are our most powerful tools. By recognizing the signs, engaging in open dialogue, and addressing misconceptions, we can offer hope and support to those in their darkest moments. The journey from passive to active ideation is not predetermined; timely intervention and compassionate care can pave a path toward healing and resilience.

1.2 Recognizing Signs in Loved Ones: Beyond the Words

When extending understanding to those we hold dear, our perceptions often extend beyond the spoken word into the realm of actions and mannerisms. The subtleties in behavior or even a slight change in routine can sometimes signal distress signals that words cannot convey. Recognizing these signs, whether they be physical or behavioral, is paramount in our efforts to provide timely support to loved ones who might be silently struggling with suicidal thoughts.

Non-Verbal Cues

Observing non-verbal cues requires a mindful approach while exercising situational awareness within the interactions of our relationships. These can manifest as changes in self-care, sleep patterns, or even a diminished interest in previously enjoyed activities. For instance, a once meticulous friend may start neglecting their appearance or personal hygiene, signaling a shift in their mental well-being. Similarly, variations in eating habits, whether a loss of appetite or an increase in binge eating, can also hint at emotional turmoil. Physical signs, such as unexplained aches, increased use of alcohol or drugs, or sudden weight changes, demand attention with an empathetic focus on understanding.

Changes in Communication

Communication, the bridge that connects us, can also reveal alterations in one's mental state. A once communicative friend, loved one, or family member may abruptly turn inward, limiting their responses to brief, single-word answers or sidestepping interactions entirely. Conversely, an abrupt increase in communication, particularly messages that hint at goodbye or carry a tone of finality, should raise immediate concern. These subtle or stark shifts serve as red flags or warning signs, urging us to reach out and offer a supportive presence.

The Role of Intuition

Intuition, often termed our inner compass or "gut instincts," can be crucial in alerting us to unspoken distress in those we are close to. This innate sense can signal when something isn't quite right, even when, outwardly, everything appears normal. Trusting in this intuition means acknowledging that we might be subconsciously picking up on distress cues that are not overtly visible. It underscores the importance of our emotional connections, enabling us to detect signs of suffering that might otherwise go unnoticed. It's that gut feeling that something is "off" when a loved one insists they're "fine."

To hone this intuition, it helps to be fully present during in-person and digital interactions. Paying close attention to what is said, how it's said, and what remains unsaid can provide valuable insights into a loved one's mental and emotional state. It's about reading between the lines and trusting your gut when it tells you someone might need help.

Creating Open Dialogues

Opening a dialogue about mental health, especially when we suspect someone might be contemplating suicide, is delicate but also imperative. The approach should be rooted in compassion, non-judgment, and patience. Here are some strategies to initiate these important conversations:

- **Choose the Right Moment**: Look for a quiet, private setting where you won't be interrupted. Creating an appropriate setting can profoundly influence the progression of the dialogue and the comfort level experienced throughout the conversation.
- **Use Open-Ended Questions**: Start with general, open-ended questions like, "I've noticed you've been going through a tough time lately. Do you want to talk about it?" This approach invites them to share without feeling cornered or defensive.
- **Express Concern Without Assumptions**: Make it clear that your concern comes from a place of love. Avoid assumptions or accusations. Phrases like, "I've noticed you haven't been yourself lately, and I'm worried about you" show care without placing blame.
- **Be Ready to Listen**: Once the conversation starts, your role primarily shifts to listening. Showing that you are there to hear them out without interrupting or offering

unsolicited advice can provide the comfort they need to open up.
- **Offer Support, Not Solutions**: It's natural to want to fix things, but sometimes, the best support is to be there and to listen. Offer to help them find professional support, but respect their pace and readiness to seek help.

Opening a dialogue about mental health can feel daunting, but it's a critical step in providing support. It's about offering a safe space for loved ones to express their feelings and fears, knowing they're not alone in their struggles. By observing non-verbal cues, recognizing changes in communication, trusting our intuition, and learning how to initiate open, supportive conversations, we can make a significant difference in the lives of those who might be silently suffering.

1.3 The Role of Mental Illness in Suicidal Ideation

Grasping the complex interplay between mental illness and suicidal thoughts is essential. Mental health conditions significantly influence one's vulnerability to contemplating suicide. However, it's imperative to approach this topic with sensitivity and a commitment to dispelling myths that foster stigma.

Common Mental Health Conditions Linked

Several mental health disorders are frequently associated with an elevated risk of experiencing suicidal thoughts. Among these, depression stands out due to its profound impact on an individual's mood, outlook on life, and motivation, often leading to feelings of hopelessness. Bipolar disorder, characterized by extreme mood swings, can also increase the risk, especially during depressive episodes or mixed states. Anxiety disorders, including generalized anxiety disorder, panic disorder, and PTSD, contribute to heightened stress levels, which may exacerbate suicidal ideation. Additionally, mental health conditions such as schizophrenia and personality disorders, with an emphasis on borderline personality disorder, are recognized for their association with heightened suicide risk. The severe emotional distress and disorientation these disorders provoke primarily create this connection.

Misrepresentation in Media

The portrayal of mental illness and suicide in the media often falls short of capturing the complex reality and context of suicidal ideation, resulting in pervasive misunderstandings. Films and television shows sometimes depict these issues through sensationalized or overly simplistic lenses, contributing to misunderstanding and stigma. For instance, characters with mental illness are frequently shown as inherently dangerous or as if their conditions inevitably lead to suicide. This portrayal not only misrepresents the reality of living with mental health conditions but also discourages people from seeking help due to fear of judgment. Media creators must seek guidance from mental health professionals when depicting these issues to ensure accuracy and sensitivity.

Understanding vs. Stigmatizing

Distinguishing between understanding mental illness as a factor in suicidal ideation and stigmatizing those who suffer from these conditions needs to be a priority. Acknowledging that mental health disorders can increase the risk of suicide does not imply that everyone with a mental illness will experience suicidal thoughts. Nor should it lead to treating individuals with mental illness differently. Education plays a vital role in shifting perspectives from stigmatization to understanding. By learning about the complexities of mental health conditions and the experiences of those affected, society can foster a more inclusive and supportive environment. It's about recognizing mental illnesses as health conditions that require care and compassion, not judgment.

Treatment and Support

For individuals living with mental health conditions, accessing effective treatment and support is critical to managing their symptoms and reducing the risk of suicidal ideation. Treatment options vary depending on the specific disorder but often include a combination of medication, therapy, and lifestyle adjustments. For example:

- **Medication**: Antidepressants, mood stabilizers, and antipsychotics can help manage symptoms of various mental health conditions. Individuals need to work closely with their healthcare providers to find the proper medication and dosage.
- **Therapy**: Psychotherapy, such as cognitive-behavioral therapy (CBT) and dialectical behavior therapy (DBT), has been shown to be effective in treating conditions like depression, anxiety disorders, and borderline personality disorder. These therapies can provide individuals with coping strategies and tools to manage their symptoms.
- **Support Groups**: Participating in support groups can offer a sense of community and understanding. Sharing experiences and coping strategies with others with similar conditions can reduce feelings of isolation.
- **Lifestyle Adjustments**: Regular physical activity, a balanced diet, and sufficient sleep can improve overall well-being and support mental health.

For many, a combination of these approaches yields the best outcomes. It's also essential for individuals to have a strong, established support system, including friends, family, and mental health professionals, who can provide encouragement and assistance throughout their treatment journey.

Access to care remains a significant barrier for many people living with mental health conditions. Efforts to increase awareness, reduce stigma, and improve mental health services are essential for ensuring that everyone has the opportunity to receive the support they need. This includes advocating for mental health coverage in healthcare plans, increasing funding for mental health services, and promoting education about mental health in schools and communities.

In sum, recognizing the role of mental illness in suicidal ideation requires a balanced approach that emphasizes understanding, compassion, and access to comprehensive care. By addressing the misconceptions and barriers associated with mental health conditions, society can move towards a more supportive and inclusive environment for all individuals.

1.4 Debunking Myths: What Suicidal Ideation Does and Doesn't Mean

It is clear that myths and misconceptions not only cloud public understanding regarding suicidal ideation but also hinder effective and adequate support for those in need. By confronting these myths head-on, we can foster a more informed and compassionate approach to aiding those experiencing suicidal thoughts.

Suicidal Ideation as a Cry for Help

The notion that suicidal ideation is merely an attempt to seek attention undermines the gravity of what individuals are experiencing. Far from a bid for attention, expressing suicidal thoughts often represents a critical juncture where an individual feels so overwhelmed by their pain that they see no other way to communicate their distress. It's a signal that they need help, understanding, and support, not judgment. Acknowledging and responding to these expressions with genuine concern can be the first step in showing someone that there are other options and that people care about their well-being.

Indication of Deep Pain

Suicidal thoughts are a manifestation of deep emotional or psychological pain. It's a pain so consuming that the individual cannot see a future beyond it. This pain can originate from numerous sources, including mental health disorders, traumatic incidents, or significant alterations in life circumstances. Such changes may encompass relationship shifts like breakups or divorces, the death of someone close, legal challenges, financial troubles, job loss, and other similar events. It's critical to recognize that such thoughts are not a character flaw or a weakness but a sign that someone is struggling to cope with intense feelings or situations. Understanding this can shift the conversation from one of judgment to one of empathy and support.

Not Inevitable

Another common misconception is that suicidal thoughts inevitably lead to suicide attempts. This fatalistic view overlooks the crucial role of intervention and support in altering this trajectory. With timely and appropriate help, many individuals find ways to cope with their pain, rediscover hope, and rebuild their desire to live. It's important to stress that thoughts of suicide are often temporary and situational, with many individuals never acting on these thoughts, especially if they receive the support they need.

The Importance of Taking All Signs Seriously

Every expression of suicidal thought, no matter how subtle, warrants serious attention and empathy. Dismissing or minimizing these signs can have devastating consequences. Friends, family, and professionals must treat any mention of suicide with the utmost concern. This doesn't mean panicking or overreacting but approaching the individual with care, offering a listening ear, and guiding them toward professional help. This approach reinforces the message that their feelings are valid, their life has value, and there is hope for feeling better.

Each of these myths serves as a barrier to understanding and supporting individuals grappling with suicidal thoughts. By debunking these misconceptions, we can create a society that approaches suicidality with the seriousness, empathy, and compassion it deserves. This shift in perspective is crucial in changing the perception of help-seeking behaviors and building a world where those in pain feel supported in seeking help and finding paths toward healing.

1.5 The Impact of Social Media: A Double-Edged Sword

In the digital age, social media has woven itself into the fabric of daily life, shaping our interactions, perceptions, and even our feelings of self-worth. Its omnipresence means that it inevitably plays a role in the landscape of mental health, acting as both a potential source of harm and a beacon of support.

The Negative Influence

For many, the curated perfection displayed on social media platforms can amplify feelings of isolation and inadequacy. The constant barrage of images and updates showcasing others' success, happiness, and social connections can distort reality, making one's own life seem dull or inadequate by comparison. This phenomenon, often referred to as "comparisonitis," can lead to a downward spiral of self-doubt and loneliness.

Moreover, the anonymity and distance afforded by online interactions can sometimes bring out the worst in people, leading to cyberbullying or hateful comments that can deeply affect someone already struggling with mental health issues. The impact of these negative interactions can be profound, reinforcing feelings of isolation and unworthiness.

Potential for Support and Connection

Conversely, social media holds immense potential as a source of support and connection for those feeling isolated. Numerous groups and communities exist across various platforms, offering spaces for individuals to share their experiences, challenges, and triumphs with mental health. For someone struggling silently, discovering a community of people with similar experiences can be a lifeline, offering a sense of belonging and understanding that might be missing in their offline life.

Personal stories of struggle and recovery, shared openly on social media, can also serve as powerful beacons of hope for those grappling with their mental health challenges. Seeing someone else articulate feelings and thoughts similar to their own can validate their experiences and inspire them to seek help or persevere through tough times.

Navigating Online Spaces Safely

Given the dual nature of social media's impact, navigating these platforms in a way that safeguards mental health is crucial. Here are some strategies for engaging with social media constructively:

- **Curate Your Feed**: Actively manage who you follow and what content you engage with. Prioritize accounts and groups that uplift and support your mental well-being while unfollowing or muting those that contribute to negative feelings.
- **Set Boundaries**: Limit daily time spent on social media use. Designate "social media-free" times, especially during periods meant for relaxation or right before bedtime, to mitigate its impact on your mental health and sleep quality.
- **Engage Mindfully**: Before posting or commenting, pause to consider the intent and potential impact. Engage in ways that foster positivity and understanding, and avoid getting drawn into arguments or negative exchanges.
- **Seek Real Connections**: Use social media as a starting point for forming real-world connections. Join online groups or communities with shared interests and look for opportunities to engage offline through meetups or events.

By approaching social media intentionally, individuals can minimize its potential harms while maximizing its support and connection.

Social Media as an Educational Tool

Beyond individual use, social media platforms present a valuable opportunity for spreading awareness and education about suicide prevention. With their extensive reach, these platforms can break down barriers to information and destigmatize discussions around mental health.

Organizations and advocates can leverage social media to share accurate information about mental health conditions, suicide warning signs, and resources for help. Educational campaigns can be amplified through hashtags, shares, and influencer partnerships, reaching broad audiences and fostering a more informed and supportive community.

Interactive elements, such as live Q&A sessions with mental health professionals or webinars on coping strategies, further enhance social media's educational potential. These initiatives provide valuable information and model open and healthy discussions about mental health, encouraging individuals to seek help when needed.

Leveraging social media as an educational tool requires prioritizing accuracy and sensitivity. Mental health professionals should vet content to ensure it's informative, non-triggering, and supportive. By doing so, social media can transform from a potential source of harm into a powerful ally in the fight against suicide and the promotion of mental well-being.

Social media is a significant factor in navigating the complexities of mental health in the digital age. It influences how individuals perceive themselves and their connections with others. While it can exacerbate feelings of isolation and inadequacy, it offers unparalleled support, connection, and education opportunities. By engaging with social media mindfully, setting clear boundaries, and leveraging its reach for educational purposes, we can harness its potential for good, creating a more supportive and informed community for those struggling with mental health issues.

1.6 Cultural Influences on Perceptions of Suicide

Cultural contexts significantly influence how suicide is perceived and addressed worldwide, embedding unique perspectives within the fabric of each society. These cultural narratives play a pivotal role in shaping attitudes towards mental health and suicidal ideation, influencing everything from the willingness to seek help to the strategies used in offering support.

Variations Across Cultures

Across cultures, perceptions of suicide range from taboo and stigmatized to being seen through a more understanding or even romantic lens. In some societies, mental health struggles and suicide are shrouded in silence, viewed as a personal or family failure rather than a call for empathy and support. Other cultures may recognize suicidal thoughts as a symptom of societal failings, emphasizing communal responsibility over individual blame. This spectrum of understanding affects how individuals experiencing suicidal ideation perceive their struggles and their likelihood of seeking help.

For example, in many Western cultures, there's a growing movement towards destigmatization and open discussion of mental health issues, including suicide. Contrastingly, in some Asian cultures, the emphasis on collective identity and familial honor can lead to a more stigmatized view of suicide, discouraging open dialogue and potentially delaying or preventing individuals from seeking support.

Stigma and Silence

The stigma attached to suicide in many cultures acts as a formidable barrier to those in need of help. This stigma often stems from historical, religious, or societal beliefs that frame suicide as a moral failing or weakness. Such views can lead to a culture of silence around mental health, where individuals fear judgment not only for themselves but also for their families. This fear can be so pervasive that it overrides the desperate need for help, pushing those struggling with suicidal ideation further into isolation.

The silence surrounding suicide not only affects individuals' willingness to seek help but also impacts the broader community's ability to recognize and respond to signs of distress. Without open dialogue, misconceptions and myths flourish, further entrenching the stigma and making it harder for those affected to find a voice.

Cultural Competence in Support

Effectively addressing suicidal ideation requires a culturally competent approach that honors and understands the diverse backgrounds of those in need. Cultural competence in mental health support involves recognizing the influence of cultural factors on how individuals experience and express distress and how they perceive and access support.

Mental health professionals and support networks must have the knowledge and sensitivity to navigate cultural nuances. This includes understanding the potential impact of stigma within different cultures, recognizing culturally specific signs of distress, and respecting cultural expressions of pain and coping. In some cultures, people might avoid direct discussions about personal struggles, requiring support providers to be attentive to indirect expressions of distress or to utilize trusted community or family networks as part of the support process.

Developing cultural competence also involves challenging one's biases and assumptions, ensuring that support is available and perceived as accessible and acceptable by those from varied cultural backgrounds, training in cultural sensitivity, and engaging with communities to understand their needs and perspectives. These considerations are imperative for building trust and effectively reaching those in need.

Leveraging Cultural Strengths

While cultural factors can contribute to the stigma and silence surrounding suicide, they also offer unique strengths and resources for prevention and support. Many cultures have strong community and family networks that, when engaged effectively, can provide powerful support systems for individuals facing mental health challenges.

Community leaders, including religious and spiritual leaders, often hold significant influence and can play a vital role in changing perceptions of suicide and mental health. By integrating mental health education and support into community structures and utilizing culturally resonant messages of hope and resilience, these leaders can help break down barriers to seeking help.

In addition, cultural traditions and practices can offer valuable pathways for coping and healing. Mindfulness practices, storytelling, communal rituals, and other cultural expressions can provide comfort and connection for those feeling isolated by their struggles. Recognizing and incorporating these cultural resources into suicide prevention and mental health support not only honors individuals' backgrounds but also enhances the effectiveness of interventions by aligning them with familiar and meaningful practices.

In navigating the complex interplay between culture and perceptions of suicide, it becomes clear that a nuanced, respectful approach is essential. By understanding and addressing the specific cultural factors that influence perceptions of suicide and by leveraging cultural strengths and resources, we can build more inclusive, effective support systems. This approach of cultural competence plays a crucial role in dismantling the stigma and silence frequently associated with suicidal thoughts. It guarantees that the support is significant and deeply resonates with individuals from various cultural backgrounds.

1.7 Navigating Suicidal Ideation in LGBTQ+ Communities

The LGBTQ+ community faces a unique set of challenges that, unfortunately, elevate the risk of experiencing suicidal thoughts. These challenges are deeply rooted in societal discrimination and exclusion, which can lead to feelings of isolation, rejection, and despair. Recognizing the distinct experiences of LGBTQ+ individuals is crucial in offering the proper support and understanding.

Higher Risks Faced

LGBTQ+ individuals encounter societal barriers and personal conflicts that significantly impact their mental health. Whether overt or subtle, discrimination and the fear of rejection from family, friends, and society contribute to a heightened sense of vulnerability. For many, these pressures can lead to internalized homophobia, identity concealment, and profound loneliness, all of which are risk factors for suicidal ideation.

The statistics paint a stark picture; LGBTQ+ youth, for instance, are significantly more likely to consider and attempt suicide than their heterosexual peers. This disparity underscores the urgent need for targeted support and interventions that address the specific realities of the LGBTQ+ experience.

The Importance of Inclusive Support

Creating support systems that explicitly affirm LGBTQ+ identities is critical. Traditional mental health services often lack the cultural competence to address the unique challenges faced by LGBTQ+ individuals, inadvertently perpetuating feelings of isolation. Inclusive support means providers are not only aware of but sensitive to the nuances of sexual orientation and gender identity, ensuring that their practices are free from bias and discrimination.

Inclusive support also involves advocating for the rights and well-being of LGBTQ+ individuals, both within mental health settings and in broader societal contexts. This advocacy helps to create an environment where seeking help is seen as a strength, not a weakness, and where individuals feel valued and understood.

Role of Community and Acceptance

The power of community and acceptance in mitigating the risks of suicide among LGBTQ+ populations cannot be overstated. A sense of belonging, whether found in LGBTQ+ specific groups, inclusive religious communities, or supportive family structures, acts as a buffer against the adverse effects of discrimination and exclusion.

Community support offers more than just a safe haven; it provides a platform for sharing experiences, fostering resilience, and empowering individuals to embrace their identities fully. When individuals feel accepted and supported, they are more likely to seek help for mental health issues and less likely to experience suicidal thoughts.

Programs and initiatives encouraging acceptance within families, schools, and workplaces are vital. Education plays a key role here, challenging stereotypes and prejudices while promoting understanding and empathy. When we weave acceptance into the fabric of our communities, we create a healthier environment for all, particularly for those who identify as LGBTQ+.

Creating Safe Spaces

Safe spaces, both physical and virtual, are essential for LGBTQ+ individuals to explore and express their identities without fear of judgment or harm. These spaces offer a refuge from daily discrimination, providing opportunities for connection, support, and validation.

Creating these spaces requires a conscious effort to foster inclusivity and respect. This can include:

- **Training staff and volunteers** in LGBTQ+ cultural competency to ensure they are equipped to provide appropriate and sensitive support.
- **Implementing anti-discrimination policies** that explicitly protect LGBTQ+ individuals and create an environment where respect and dignity are non-negotiable.
- **Offering specialized resources and programs** tailored to the needs of the LGBTQ+ community, such as support groups, counseling services, and educational workshops.

- **Promoting visibility and representation** within organizations and initiatives to signal to LGBTQ+ individuals that they are welcome and valued community members.

Beyond organizational efforts, each of us has a role in creating safe spaces in our daily interactions. This means being mindful of the language we use, challenging homophobic and transphobic remarks, and showing up as allies who are willing to listen, learn, and support.

For LGBTQ+ individuals navigating suicidal ideation, these safe spaces can be lifesaving. They offer a sense of belonging, an opportunity to be seen and heard, and, most importantly, a reminder that they are not alone. Safe spaces shine as beacons of hope and acceptance in a hostile world.

As we strive to support those within the LGBTQ+ community facing suicidal thoughts, our approach must be multifaceted. It requires a commitment to inclusivity, an understanding of the unique challenges faced, and a dedication to creating environments where everyone can seek help without fear. Through targeted support, community acceptance, and the cultivation of safe spaces, we can make significant strides in reducing the risk of suicide among LGBTQ+ individuals. This effort benefits those directly affected and enriches our society as a whole, fostering a culture of understanding, acceptance, and compassion.

1.8 Veterans and Suicidal Thoughts: A Closer Look at PTSD

Veterans often carry the weight of experiences that are difficult for those outside the military to grasp fully. Transitioning from active duty to civilian life can exacerbate these challenges, sometimes leading to isolation, alienation, and misunderstanding. Among the mental health issues that Veterans may face, Post-Traumatic Stress Disorder (PTSD) is particularly significant for its potential to increase the risk of suicidal ideation.

The Link Between PTSD and Suicide

PTSD, a condition that can develop after a person has experienced or witnessed life-threatening events, is notably prevalent among veterans due to the nature of military service. The symptoms of PTSD, including intrusive memories, heightened vigilance, and emotional numbing, significantly impact a veteran's daily life and psychological well-being. This distress can often lead to suicidal thoughts as individuals struggle to cope with the aftermath of trauma.

The relationship between PTSD and suicidal ideation is complex and multifaceted. PTSD can disrupt a person's ability to regulate emotions, leading to impulsive or risky behaviors. The condition can also hinder one's capacity to connect with others, increasing feelings of loneliness and despair. For many veterans, the challenge of reconciling their military experiences with civilian life amplifies these effects, making it crucial to address PTSD as a core component of suicide prevention efforts among this population.

Understanding the Veteran Experience

To effectively support veterans, it is vital to acknowledge the unique aspects of the military experience that contribute to their mental health struggles. These include, but are not limited to:

- **Exposure to Combat**: Many veterans have faced life-threatening situations, witnessed the death of comrades, or experienced injuries themselves. These traumatic events can leave lasting psychological scars.
- **Moral Injury**: Veterans may struggle with guilt or shame related to their actions or decisions during service, contributing to emotional distress and suicidal thoughts.
- **Transition Stress**: Adjusting to civilian life presents challenges, from finding employment to reconnecting with family and friends.
- **Stigma Around Seeking Help**: Within the military culture, there's often an emphasis on strength and resilience, which can discourage individuals from seeking help for mental health issues.
- Losing the structured military environment can leave some feeling adrift and unsupported.

Understanding these factors is essential for providing empathetic and practical support to Veterans. It requires acknowledging the breadth of their experiences and the impact these can have on their mental health.

Access to Support Services

Accessible, veteran-specific mental health services are critical for addressing the high rates of PTSD and suicidal ideation among veterans. While resources like the Veterans Affairs (VA) health system exist, barriers to access and utilization remain. These barriers may include long wait times, geographical limitations, and a perceived lack of understanding from providers about military culture.

Improving access to support services involves several key strategies:

- **Expanding Telehealth Options**: This can make mental health services more accessible to Veterans living in remote areas or those with mobility issues.
- **Increasing Awareness of Services**: Many veterans may not be aware of the mental health resources available to them. Outreach and education efforts are essential for closing this gap.
- **Training Providers in Military Cultural Competency**: Organizations should train mental health professionals to understand Veterans' unique experiences and needs to offer more effective support.
- **Peer Support Programs**: Veteran-led support groups offer a space where individuals can share their experiences with others who genuinely understand, fostering a sense of community and belonging.

By enhancing the availability and quality of mental health services tailored to Veterans, we can better address the root causes of PTSD and suicidal ideation, offering hope and pathways to healing.

The Role of Community and Validation

Validation of a veteran's experiences by their community can significantly impact their sense of belonging and self-worth. Communities can contribute to this sense of validation through:

- **Public Recognition**: Community events that honor Veterans' service and sacrifices help to affirm the value of their contributions to society.

- **Educational Initiatives**: Programs that educate the public about Veterans' challenges can foster greater understanding and empathy, reducing stigma and isolation.
- **Volunteer Opportunities**: Engaging Veterans in volunteer work or community projects can provide a sense of purpose and connection, counteracting feelings of alienation.

Moreover, validation from fellow veterans and military community members can be particularly impactful. Peer support initiatives that connect Veterans offer an environment where their experiences are inherently understood and respected. These connections can be a powerful antidote to the loneliness and disconnection that contribute to suicidal thoughts.

In conclusion, addressing the complex relationship between PTSD and suicidal ideation among Veterans requires a multifaceted approach. It involves understanding the unique challenges of the Veteran experience, improving access to tailored mental health services, and fostering a supportive community environment. Through these efforts, we can offer Veterans the support and validation they need to navigate the difficult transition to civilian life and find pathways to healing and hope.

1.9 Suicidal Ideation in Adolescents: Understanding the Teenage Mind

Adolescence is fraught with distinct challenges for teenagers and their guardians alike, marking a period of intense growth and vulnerability. Given that the adolescent brain is still developing, it perceives emotions and evaluates risks in ways distinct from those of an adult brain. This difference contributes to greater vulnerability during these pivotal years.

The Impact of Adolescent Brain Development

During adolescence, the brain undergoes significant changes that influence emotional regulation and risk assessment. The prefrontal cortex, responsible for decision-making and impulse control, matures faster than the amygdala, which processes emotions. This imbalance can result in intense emotional experiences and impulsive decisions, including risky behaviors or considering self-harm as a solution to emotional pain. Understanding the significant developmental differences between adolescent and adult brains is essential for adults who aim to support teenagers effectively. This understanding illuminates the sometimes baffling reactions of adolescents to stress or conflict, offering a clearer perspective on their unique challenges.

Social Pressures and Expectations

Teenagers today face an array of social pressures and expectations that can feel overwhelming. Academic demands, social dynamics, and familial expectations converge and all pile-up, creating a perfect storm of stress that can lead to feelings of inadequacy and hopelessness. Social media amplifies these pressures, presenting an idealized version of life that is difficult to live up to. For some teens, these pressures can exacerbate underlying mental health issues, leading to suicidal ideation. Recognizing the sources of these pressures and the impact they have on adolescent mental health is the first step in offering meaningful support.

- **Academic Pressure**: The push to excel in school and prepare for a successful future can be a significant source of stress, leading to anxiety and depression if teens feel they can't meet these expectations.

- **Social Dynamics**: Navigating friendships and romantic relationships, often while dealing with bullying or social isolation, adds another layer of emotional complexity.
- **Familial Expectations**: Striving to meet parents' or caregivers' expectations, especially when they conflict with a teen's own desires or identity, can also create internal turmoil.

Effective Communication Strategies

Opening lines of communication with adolescents about their mental health and emotional well-being requires patience, understanding, and strategy. Here are some approaches that foster open dialogue:

- **Active Listening**: Show genuine interest in what they have to say without immediately jumping to solutions or judgments. This approach cultivates an atmosphere of transparency, encouraging ongoing dialogues that can contribute to a sense of security and ease.
- **Validation**: Acknowledge their feelings and experiences as valid. Teens need to feel understood and accepted, not dismissed.
- **Open-Ended Questions**: Ask questions that can't be answered with a simple yes or no to encourage deeper conversation. For example, try asking, "What has been on your mind lately?"
- **Non-Verbal Cues**: Pay attention to body language and other non-verbal signals that might indicate distress, as teens might not always express their feelings in words.

The Role of Schools in Prevention

Schools play a pivotal role in the early identification and support of students at risk of suicidal ideation. With most teenagers spending a significant portion of their day in school, educators and school staff are uniquely positioned to observe changes in behavior and intervene when necessary. Here are several ways schools can actively participate in suicide prevention:

- **Training Staff**: Educate teachers, counselors, and administrative staff on the signs of suicidal ideation and the best practices for intervention. This training ensures that staff can respond appropriately to student mental health concerns.
- **Creating Supportive Environments**: Foster a school culture where students feel safe discussing mental health concerns. Schools can achieve this culture through regular mental health awareness programs, peer support groups, and clear policies on bullying and discrimination.
- **Early Intervention Programs**: Implement screening and referral programs to identify at-risk students and connect them with the appropriate local support services within and outside the school.
- **Engagement with Parents and Caregivers**: Schools should work closely with families, providing them with information on how to support their teenager's mental health and when to seek professional help.

Recognizing the distinct challenges teens encounter, ranging from brain development to societal pressures and the need for nurturing and effective communication, empowers caregivers and professionals to offer vital support during these formative years. This comprehensive approach not only aids in navigating the complexities of adolescent mental health but also provides a foundation for resilience and well-being that can last into adulthood.

1.10 Addressing Suicidal Ideation in the Elderly: Loneliness and Beyond

The golden years, often portrayed as a serene and fulfilling stage of life, can sometimes cast long shadows of loneliness and isolation, particularly as social circles diminish and physical health wanes. For the elderly, these factors can significantly heighten the risk of suicidal ideation, marking a pressing need for attentive care and understanding from those around them.

The Role of Loneliness

Isolation and loneliness can serve as significant triggers for suicidal thoughts in the elderly. With advancing age, individuals often encounter the loss of a spouse, friends, or their autonomy, leading to a profound sense of loneliness that transcends simple emotional discomfort and touches on existential concerns. These feelings can be exacerbated by physical limitations or conditions like dementia, which further isolate the individual from their surroundings and loved ones. It's a stark reality that, despite living in an era of unparalleled connectivity, many elderly individuals find themselves tangled in the grips of solitude, significantly impacting their desire to engage with the world around them.

Recognizing Signs in Elderly Loved Ones

Spotting the signs of suicidal ideation in older adults requires a keen and compassionate eye, as they might not always express their distress as directly as younger individuals might. Some indicators can include:

- Withdrawal from social activities they once enjoyed, signaling a deeper issue than mere disinterest.
- Verbal cues that hint at despair include frequent talks about the burden they feel they pose to others or a desire to escape their loneliness.
- Neglecting personal care or previously upheld routines might suggest a diminishing concern for their well-being.
- A sudden preoccupation with death or giving away cherished possessions, possibly indicating they are contemplating their mortality or considering suicide.

Understanding these signs can help initiate timely conversations and interventions that can steer them away from the path of despair.

Challenges in Accessing Mental Health Care

The stigmatization of mental health issues among older generations and logistical hurdles compound the unique challenges the elderly face in accessing mental health care. Growing up in an era when people rarely discussed mental health, many older adults have developed an ingrained reluctance to seek help for emotional or psychological distress. Furthermore, physical limitations or lack of transportation can hinder them from attending appointments or accessing services. This issue intensifies within a healthcare system that often prioritizes physical health over mental well-being, insufficiently addressing the emotional and psychological needs of the elderly.

Creating a Network of Support

Establishing strong support networks is crucial for protecting the mental well-being of older adults. This network extends beyond the family unit to encompass healthcare providers, community resources, and peers. It's about creating a multidimensional support system that addresses their emotional and psychological needs as well as social and practical aspects. Here are some ways to build this network:

- **Family and Friends**: Encourage regular check-ins and visits and involve them in activities that foster a sense of belonging and purpose. Simple acts of inclusion can significantly improve their perceived quality of life.
- **Healthcare Providers**: Establish open lines of communication with doctors, nurses, and mental health professionals who can monitor their health, offer necessary interventions, and provide guidance to families on how to support their elderly loved ones effectively.
- **Community Resources**: Leverage local community centers, religious organizations, and senior centers offering programs and activities for older adults. These can range from exercise classes to art workshops to reduce isolation and promote engagement.
- **Technology**: Introduce them to technology that can help bridge the distance between them and their loved ones through video calls or social media. Training sessions provided by community centers or family members can empower older adults to use these tools confidently.

Building this network requires patience, persistence, and creativity, but its impact on an elderly individual's life is immeasurable. It's about weaving a safety net that not only catches them when they fall but also lifts them, reminding them of their valued place in the tapestry of life.

TWO

Cultivating Mindfulness and Emotional Resilience

I magine holding a glass of water filled to the brim. The world around you blurs as you focus solely on not spilling it. This singular focus, in essence, mirrors the practice of mindfulness—

being fully present in the moment, undistracted by the myriad thoughts that usually occupy our minds. This chapter guides you through mindfulness, revealing its power as a practice and a transformative tool for mental and emotional well-being.

2.1 Grounding in the Present

Mindfulness roots us firmly in the present, serving as an anchor that prevents the mind from drifting into worries about the future or ruminations about the past. Consider the act of taking a walk. Instead of getting lost in a whirlwind of thoughts, focus on the sensation of your feet touching the ground, the rhythm of your breath, and the sounds surrounding you. This simple shift in focus can significantly reduce feelings of anxiety and stress, providing a sense of calm and balance and creating some temporary distance and breathing room from the constant mental stressors faced throughout your day.

Enhancing Emotional Awareness

By cultivating mindfulness, we become more attuned to our emotional states and the triggers that influence them. It's akin to observing clouds as they pass across the sky—acknowledging their presence without becoming enveloped by them. This heightened awareness allows us to recognize and name our emotions, providing a crucial first step in managing them effectively. For instance, acknowledging "I'm feeling overwhelmed" enables us to address this emotion directly through self-care practices or seeking support rather than allowing it to dictate our actions unconsciously.

- **Daily Check-ins**: Set aside a few minutes each day to check in with yourself. Ask yourself, "How am I feeling right now?" and "What's occupying my mind now?" This practice fosters an ongoing awareness of your emotional state.

Personal Resilience

Personal resilience holds a significant role in the realm of suicide prevention and awareness, serving as a vital asset in strengthening one's inner resolve to combat vulnerabilities and address suicidal thoughts. Experts often define personal resilience as the capacity to bounce back from adversity, confront challenges head-on, and maintain a sense of purpose and optimism even in life's darkest moments.

In the context of suicide prevention, personal resilience acts as a cornerstone, equipping individuals with the mental fortitude needed to navigate through moments of despair, hopelessness, and intense emotional turmoil. By fostering personal resilience through practices such as mindfulness and self-reflection, individuals can gain a deeper insight into their emotional landscape and nurture a heightened self-awareness and effective coping mechanisms to confront negative thoughts and impulses.

Mindfulness as a Daily Practice

Incorporating mindfulness into daily routines doesn't require special equipment or vast stretches of time. It's about weaving moments of awareness into the fabric of your day.

- **Mindful Eating**: Turn meals into an opportunity for mindfulness by eating slowly and savoring each bite, paying attention to the flavors, textures, and sensations. This will help you be mentally present in the moment you are experiencing.
- **Breathing Exercises**: Practice focused breathing exercises, like the 4-7-8 technique, to center your attention and reduce stress. Breathe in for four counts, hold for seven, and exhale for eight.
- **Gratitude Journaling**: End your day by jotting down three things you're grateful for. This intentional practice shifts focus to positive experiences, fostering a sense of contentment and helping to create positive mental routines.

Evidence-Based Benefits

The research underscores the profound impact of mindfulness on psychological resilience. Studies have shown that regular mindfulness practice can reduce stress, anxiety, and depression. It enhances our capacity to cope with adversity, making us less reactive to stressors and more adept at navigating challenges. For instance, a study published in the *Journal of Clinical Psychology* found that mindfulness-based interventions significantly reduced symptoms of anxiety and depression among participants.

Mindfulness also bolsters our ability to enjoy life, appreciate the present moment, and fully engage with the world. It's a tool that supports mental health and enriches our daily experiences, allowing us to lead more balanced and fulfilling lives.

As we delve deeper into the practices that fortify our mental and emotional resilience, mindfulness stands out as a technique and a way of living. It's about engaging fully with the present, nurturing awareness, and embracing life with openness and curiosity. This chapter has outlined practical steps to integrate mindfulness into daily life, offering a pathway to enhanced mental well-being and a deeper connection with the world around you.

Grounding yourself in the present, enhancing your emotional awareness, and making mindfulness a daily practice can help you embark on a journey toward greater peace, resilience, and joy. The evidence-based benefits of mindfulness underscore its efficacy as a tool for mental health, providing a solid foundation for navigating the challenges and complexities of life with grace and equanimity.

2.2 The Power of Positive Thinking: Reshaping Your Narrative

Thoughts create patterns in our minds that influence how we see the world. These patterns are sometimes filled with shadows, casting our outlook in negativity. However, we possess the extraordinary capacity to change this narrative by weaving positive, hopeful threads into our mental fabric. This section delves into the transformative power of positive thinking in altering our emotional and psychological perspectives.

Shifting Perspectives

Shifting our perspective is like changing the lens through which we see our existence. It involves deliberately choosing to see the light of optimism amid life's darker moments. This doesn't mean we ignore our struggles; instead, we focus on the valuable lessons and opportunities they bring. For example, a setback at work isn't perceived as just a failure; it's an opportunity to develop our skills and resilience. By reshaping how we perceive such experiences, we nurture a mindset that views challenges as opportunities for personal development and growth rather than insurmountable obstacles—essentially turning lemons into lemonade by finding growth in adversity.

To practice this shift:

- Reflect on a recent challenge and list its positive outcomes or learnings.
- Actively acknowledge the silver linings in daily situations, no matter how small.

Cognitive Restructuring Techniques

Cognitive restructuring, a fundamental aspect of cognitive-behavioral therapy (CBT), provides a structured approach to recognizing and altering detrimental thought patterns. This method starts with becoming aware of the automatic negative thoughts that frequently cross our minds during challenging times. We then challenge these thoughts, scrutinizing their accuracy and helpfulness. Finally, we replace them with more balanced, positive affirmations that more accurately reflect reality.

Consider the thought, "I'll never be good at this." Through cognitive restructuring, we might challenge this by asking, "Is it that I'll never be good, or do I just need more practice?" The replacement thought could be, "With time and effort, I can improve."

To start this process:

- Keep a thought journal, noting down negative thoughts as they arise.
- Challenge these thoughts by questioning their validity and looking for evidence contradicting them.
- Replace them with more positive, realistic statements.

Building a Positive Self-Image

Our internal dialogues often shape our self-image for better or worse. Positive affirmations and self-talk act as nourishing rain on the seeds of our self-esteem, encouraging them to bloom. Simple affirmations like, "I am capable and resilient," or "I grow stronger with every challenge" remind us of our worth and potential. Repeating these affirmations, especially during moments of doubt or criticism, reinforces a positive self-image and bolsters our resilience against life's storms.

To cultivate positive self-talk:

- Create a list of positive affirmations that resonate with you.
- Recite these affirmations daily, particularly during moments of stress or self-doubt.
- Place affirmations in frequently visited areas, such as your desk or workplace, using sticky notes for visibility where appropriate. This ensures regular exposure to positive messages, fostering the internalization of optimism.
- Visualize yourself embodying these affirmations, experiencing the confidence and strength they invoke.

Case Studies

Real-life examples illuminate the profound impact of positive thinking on individuals' lives. Consider the story of Alex, who, after a difficult divorce, found himself mired in negativity and despair. Alex gradually shifted his perspective by engaging in cognitive restructuring and daily affirmations. He began to view the end of his marriage not as a failure but as an opportunity for personal growth and new beginnings. This shift didn't happen overnight, but through consistent effort, Alex transformed his outlook, improving his mental health and opening the door to new relationships and experiences.

Another case is that of Samantha, a young professional who struggled with impostor syndrome, where individuals doubt their accomplishments and have a persistent internalized fear of being exposed as a "fraud." Despite external evidence of their competence, individuals often experiencing imposter syndrome attribute their success to luck or deception rather than their abilities. Despite her achievements, she was plagued by the belief that she wasn't genuinely competent and that her successes were just flukes. Samantha challenged these thoughts through cognitive restructuring, gathering evidence of her skills and accomplishments. She adopted affirmations that reinforced her competence and worth, significantly boosting her confidence and job performance.

These stories, among countless others, underscore the power of positive thinking in overcoming adversity, boosting self-esteem, and reshaping our life narrative. By actively focusing on positivity, challenging negative thought patterns, and building a nurturing self-dialogue, we unlock the potential to transform our emotional and psychological landscape, paving the way for a more fulfilling and resilient life.

2.3 Emotional Regulation in Times of Crisis

During times of crisis, our emotions often dictate our responses and actions, sometimes leading us astray from what's truly best for us. In these moments, mastering emotional regulation becomes essential, serving as a guiding light to steer through the turbulent waters of our thoughts and feelings. This segment delves into the core of emotional responses in crises, techniques for handling intense emotions, the crucial significance of emotional intelligence, and the enduring rewards of honing emotional regulation skills.

Understanding Emotional Responses

Crises, by their very nature, evoke strong emotional responses. These reactions, ranging from fear and anger to sadness and despair, are deeply rooted in our instinctual drive to protect ourselves. However, when emotions run high, they can cloud judgment, leading to impulsive decisions that may exacerbate the situation. Recognizing the physiological and psychological mechanisms behind these emotional responses is the first step toward managing them effectively. It's akin to understanding the mechanics of a car; with this knowledge, one gains the ability to steer it more skillfully.

- **Physiological Basis**: In times of crisis, the body activates its fight-or-flight response, releasing stress hormones that prepare us for immediate action. While this response can be life-saving in actual danger, it often overreacts to emotional stress, leading to heightened anxiety or panic.
- **Psychological Impact**: Emotionally charged situations can trigger past traumas or unresolved issues, amplifying our responses. Understanding these triggers allows for a more measured approach to managing emotions.

Strategies for Managing Intense Emotions

Mastering intense emotions in crises is not about suppression but finding balance and constructive outlets. The following strategies offer practical ways to help achieve this balance:

- **Breath Control**: When you're overwhelmed with emotions, reconnecting with your breath provides a grounding force. Deep, deliberate breathing triggers the parasympathetic nervous system, helping to combat the effects of stress and cultivate a sense of tranquility.
- **Physical Grounding Techniques**: Techniques such as holding a piece of ice or pressing your feet firmly against the ground help redirect focus from overwhelming emotions to bodily sensations, providing immediate relief from distress.
- **Identify and Label Emotions**: Naming your emotions reduces their intensity and provides clarity. This practice, known as affect labeling, engages the thinking part of the brain, reducing emotional reactivity.
- **Seek Support**: Sharing feelings with a trusted friend or professional can provide perspective, validation, and coping strategies.

The Role of Emotional Intelligence

Emotional Intelligence (EI) is critical in emotional regulation, especially during crises. It encompasses the ability to recognize, understand, and manage our emotions and those of others. Developing EI enhances our capacity to navigate emotional challenges with grace and adaptability.

- **Self-awareness**: The cornerstone of EI is self-awareness, which involves recognizing our emotional states and understanding their impact on our thoughts and behaviors. This awareness allows for more mindful responses to crises.
- **Empathy**: Developing empathy "tunes us in" to the emotions of others, empowering us to be supportive while

also enriching our emotional landscape with deeper connections and a more compassionate mindset.
- **Social Skills**: In times of crisis, effective communication and conflict resolution skills are critical elements of Emotional Intelligence (EI). They empower us to articulate our needs and worries clearly, all while acknowledging and empathetically dealing with the emotions of those involved.

Cultivating Emotional Intelligence (EI) is a journey that demands self-reflection, consistent effort, and open-mindedness to feedback. We can expedite our development by adopting reflective practices like journaling to explore our emotional encounters or welcoming constructive feedback from those we trust.

Long-Term Benefits

The practice of emotional regulation and the cultivation of emotional intelligence offer profound long-term benefits for mental health and resilience. By mastering these skills, individuals equip themselves with the tools to face not just current crises but future challenges as well.

- **Enhanced Decision-Making**: Emotional regulation allows clearer thinking, leading to more informed and beneficial decisions during stressful times.
- **Improved Relationships**: The ability to manage emotions and understand those of others leads to more robust, more empathetic connections with family, friends, and colleagues.
- **Increased Resilience**: Over time, emotional regulation builds resilience, enabling individuals to bounce back

more quickly from setbacks and maintain a positive outlook in the face of adversity.
- **Better Mental Health**: Consistent emotional regulation contributes to overall mental well-being, reducing the likelihood of anxiety, depression, and other emotional disorders.

Emotional regulation and emotional intelligence are more than just tools for navigating crises; they are integral for building and maintaining a life of stability, satisfaction, and fortitude. By understanding our emotional responses, employing strategies to manage intense emotions, developing our emotional intelligence, and embracing the long-term benefits of these practices, we position ourselves to overcome challenges and thrive amidst them.

2.4 The Importance of Self-Compassion on the Road to Resilience

In a society that frequently links personal value and self-worth to productivity and achievements, it's common to find ourselves entangled in self-judgment when we encounter obstacles or don't meet our expectations or those of others. This is where the idea of self-compassion steps in, not just as beneficial but as essential, acting as a soothing balm that heals our wounds and fosters our growth and resilience.

Defining Self-Compassion

Self-compassion is a practice that involves treating oneself with kindness, understanding, and support, especially in moments of failure or difficulty. It stands distinct from self-esteem, which often depends on our achievements or how we compare to others. Self-compassion, in contrast, is unconditional, rooted in recognizing our shared humanity and the understanding that imperfection is part of the human experience.

Self-Compassion as Self-Care

Viewing self-compassion as an integral part of self-care shifts our approach to dealing with challenges. It moves us away from harsh self-judgment and towards a more loving and forgiving stance towards ourselves. This shift alleviates emotional suffering and opens us up to learning and growth, making self-compassion a cornerstone of mental health and resilience. When we compassionately embrace our flaws and setbacks, we foster an environment where we can thrive, even in adversity.

- **Mindful Acknowledgment**: Begin by acknowledging your feelings and experiences without judgment. Recognize your emotions as valid responses to your situation.
- **Common Humanity**: Remind yourself that you're not alone in your struggles. Everyone faces setbacks and makes mistakes; it's part of being human.
- **Kindness Over Criticism**: Replace critical self-talk with words of kindness and encouragement, as you would for a dear friend.

Practical Exercises for Self-Compassion

Cultivating self-compassion can be developed through simple daily practices encouraging a more compassionate inner dialogue. These exercises strengthen your self-compassion muscles, making kindness a default response to your imperfections and struggles.

- **Self-Compassion Breaks**: When you notice you're being hard on yourself, pause briefly. Place a hand over your

heart, breathe deeply, and offer yourself words of kindness and understanding.
- **Compassion Journaling**: Dedicate a few minutes each day to write about a situation that caused you distress, focusing on treating yourself with compassion and understanding.
- **Loving-Kindness Meditation**: Practice this meditation to generate feelings of warmth and compassion toward yourself and others. Start with yourself, then gradually extend that compassion to friends, family, and even those with difficulties.

Overcoming the Inner Critic

Our inner critic can be a formidable adversary. Often, it's a voice internalized over years of conditioning, echoing societal, familial, or personal standards we feel we've failed to meet. Silencing this critic entirely may not be possible—or even desirable, as it can sometimes motivate us to achieve our goals. However, transforming its harsh judgments into constructive feedback is both achievable and beneficial.

- **Recognize the Critic**: Learn to identify when your inner critic is speaking. Its voice is usually harsh, absolute, and critical, focusing on supposed failings or inadequacies.
- **Question Its Messages**: Challenge the critic's narratives. Ask yourself whether its claims are accurate or helpful and how you can reframe them in a more positive and compassionate light.
- **Cultivate a Compassionate Voice**: Develop a compassionate voice that counters the critic. This voice is understanding, kind, and encouraging, focusing on your

efforts, growth, and learning opportunities in every situation.

Embracing self-compassion doesn't entail abandoning self-discipline or overlooking areas needing development. Instead, it involves adopting a more nurturing and empathetic approach to personal growth that recognizes our shared humanity and the complexities of living in an imperfect world. Cultivating self-compassion enhances our well-being and creates a more compassionate and empathetic global community.

These practices guide us on the journey towards nurturing self-compassion, shedding light on the path to resilience and wellness. They usher in a profound shift, moving us from self-criticism to self-advocacy and support. In doing so, we unlock the depths of our inner fortitude, empowering us to navigate life's trials with poise, bravery, and unwavering compassion for ourselves and those around us.

2.5 Setting Boundaries for Mental Health

In the intricate dance of human relationships, boundaries serve as the invisible lines that protect our emotional well-being. Just as a garden fence safeguards the blooms within, setting healthy boundaries preserves the sanctity of our mental space. This section delves into recognizing relationships that might be draining rather than enriching your life, asserting your needs effectively, and understanding how setting boundaries is a profound self-respect that lays the groundwork for resilience.

Recognizing Unhealthy Relationships

The first step in fortifying your mental health involves identifying relationships that may be detrimental. Signs of such relationships include:

- **Consistent Negativity**: Interactions often leave you feeling drained or stressed.
- **Lack of Respect for Boundaries**: Your expressed needs and limits should be addressed or routinely challenged.
- **One-sided Dynamics**: You give more attention and energy than you receive, leading to feelings of imbalance and resentment.
- **Emotional Manipulation**: Encounters often involve guilt-tripping or manipulation, making you second-guess your feelings or decisions.

Awareness of these signs empowers you to take the necessary steps to protect your mental health by modifying or limiting these interactions.

Assertiveness Training

Assertiveness is the key to communicating your needs and establishing boundaries with confidence. It involves expressing yourself openly and honestly without encroaching on the rights of others. Here are strategies to cultivate assertiveness:

- **Use "I" Statements**: Frame your needs and feelings from your perspective to avoid sounding accusatory. For example, "I feel overwhelmed when asked to take on extra tasks without notice."

- **Practice in Low-stakes Situations**: Begin asserting yourself in situations with less emotional weight to build confidence.
- **Rehearse Responses**: Anticipate potential pushback and rehearse calm, concise responses to common objections or manipulative tactics.
- **Seek Support**: Role-play scenarios with a friend or therapist to refine your assertiveness skills in a safe environment.

These techniques help establish boundaries and maintain respectful and healthy relationships.

The Role of Boundaries in Self-Respect

Establishing boundaries is a vital demonstration of self-respect. It signals to yourself and others that your needs, feelings, and time are valuable. Moreover, it:

- **Enhances Self-esteem**: You reinforce your self-esteem and confidence by asserting your worth.
- **Reduces Resentment**: Clear boundaries prevent you from overextending yourself, mitigating feelings of resentment towards others.
- **Foster's Independence**: Setting boundaries encourages others to respect your autonomy, promoting a sense of independence.

Boundaries are not barriers to intimacy but the foundations for healthy relationships. They enable you to interact with others authentically and freely, knowing your limits are respected.

Navigating Boundary Challenges

Setting and maintaining boundaries can be met with resistance, presenting challenges requiring tact and persistence. Here are solutions to common boundary-setting challenges:

- **Persistent Boundary Testing**: Consistently enforce your boundaries, even when others test them. Reiterate your needs each time someone challenges them. Reiterate your needs each time they are challenged.
- **Guilt and Self-doubt**: Remind yourself that setting boundaries is a healthy practice essential for your well-being. Revisiting your reasons for setting a particular boundary can fortify your resolve.
- **Fear of Conflict**: While asserting boundaries may initially lead to discomfort or conflict, remember that the long-term benefits to your mental health and relationships are invaluable—approach potential conflicts to find mutual understanding and respect.
- **Adjusting Boundaries as Needed**: Relationships and circumstances evolve, and so should your boundaries. Regularly assess and adjust your boundaries to reflect your current needs and situations.

In navigating these challenges, you cultivate a sense of balance in your relationships, ensuring they contribute positively to your mental health and overall well-being. Setting boundaries is not an act of selfishness but one of self-care. Honoring your needs through clear boundaries lays the groundwork for a life marked by emotional resilience and healthy, fulfilling relationships.

2.6 The Role of Physical Health in Building Resilience

The intricate dance between mind and body plays out in every aspect of our well-being. This symbiotic relationship either lifts us to health peaks or leaves us struggling in valleys of despair. The link between our physical well-being and mental fortitude is unmistakable, as every move toward physical wellness reverberates through our psychological well-being.

Connection Between Physical and Mental Health

A healthy body contributes to a strong mind. This fundamental connection, deeply embedded in our biology, transforms physical health practices from mere routines into powerful rituals that strengthen our mental and emotional resilience. Our bloodstream acts as a delivery system for nutrients, hormones, and signals, each playing a crucial role in shaping our mood, energy levels, and overall perspective on life. Physical activity, nutrition, and sleep are interconnected supportive components of our overall health.

Exercise as a Resilience Tool

Envision each step taken during a run, not just as a move towards physical fitness but as a stride towards mental fortitude. In its various forms, exercise acts as a catalyst for releasing endorphins, our body's natural mood elevators. These biochemical allies combat stress and pain, offering a sense of well-being throughout our daily lives. The discipline and routine of regular physical activity also mirror the structure and resilience needed to face life's challenges.

To incorporate exercise into your life:

- **Consistency Over Intensity**: A short daily walk trumps sporadic intense workouts. Aim for regularity to build a sustainable habit.
- **Find What You Enjoy**: Engaging in an activity you love increases the likelihood of sticking with it, whether it's yoga, swimming, or dancing.
- **Set Realistic Goals**: Small, achievable goals foster a sense of accomplishment and motivate continued effort.

Nutrition and Mental Health

The adage "You are what you eat" holds profound truths when considering mental health. Balanced nutrition acts as fuel not just for the body but also for the mind. Omega-3 fatty acids, found in fish, flaxseeds, and walnuts, are champions for brain health, supporting cognitive functions and mood regulation. Vitamins and minerals from a colorful array of fruits and vegetables combat oxidative stress that can lead to mood disorders. Viewing food as nourishment for both body and mind encourages choices that support overall well-being.

Tips for a balanced diet:

- **Diverse Plate**: Aim for various colors and types of food in your meals to ensure a wide range of nutrients.
- **Mindful Eating**: Pay attention to your hunger cues and eat without distractions to improve digestion and satisfaction.
- **Hydration**: Adequate water intake is crucial for brain function and mood regulation. As a general guideline, aim for eight glasses a day.

Sleep Hygiene Practices

Sleep, often underrated in our fast-paced society, is the cornerstone of physical and mental health. During these quiet hours of rest, our bodies repair, our memories consolidate, and our emotions balance. Poor sleep hygiene disrupts these processes, leading to heightened stress, irritability, and vulnerability to mental health disorders. Establishing a calming pre-sleep routine, maintaining a regular sleep schedule, and creating a restful environment are pivotal steps in ensuring the restorative sleep our bodies and minds require.

To improve sleep hygiene:

- **Consistent Schedule**: Going to bed and waking up simultaneously daily sets your body's internal clock, enhancing sleep quality.
- **Wind-Down Routine**: Engage in relaxing activities an hour before bed to signal your body that it's time to wind down.
- **Optimize Your Sleep Environment**: Ensure your bedroom is conducive to sleep—cool, dark, and quiet.

By integrating the principles of consistent exercise, nutritional balance, and quality sleep into our daily lives, we lay the foundation for improved overall physical health. This foundation nurtures our bodily well-being and fortifies our mental and emotional strength. Embracing this holistic strategy highlights the deep synergy between our physical habits and mental resilience, shedding light on the journey to a life marked by resilience and fulfillment.

2.7 Finding Purpose After Loss

Following a loss, our surroundings may appear void of color, the future shrouded in the fog of grief and mourning. However, within these moments of despair, opportunities for significant personal development and finding new paths emerge. This section explores strategies for reinterpreting loss, fostering personal development from trauma, aligning our actions with our core beliefs, and drawing inspiration from stories of transformation.

Reframing Loss

Reframing loss requires a transformative shift in how we perceive our experiences. It's not solely about the void that loss creates but also about appreciating the lasting aspects of our lives and the possibility of new beginnings. This approach acknowledges the depth of our sorrow while weaving it into a larger narrative of resilience and growth. It helps us see that, even in our darkest hours, there are sparks of hope and the potential for renewal, subtly indicating that our stories of strength and development continue.

- **Acceptance and Meaning**: Begin by accepting the reality of the loss, allowing yourself to feel the pain, and asking, "What can I learn from this? How can this make me stronger?"
- **Seeking Silver Linings**: Look for any positive outcomes that have emerged from your loss experience. It may have brought you closer to others, taught you something about yourself, or inspired a new passion. This perspective reaffirms that while identifying positive aspects does not diminish the sorrow associated with loss, it allows for

framing such experiences as valuable lessons that can contribute to future emotional strength and resilience.

Post-traumatic growth refers to the positive psychological change experienced as a result of struggling with highly challenging life circumstances. This growth manifests in several key areas:

- **Personal Strength**: Discovering inner reserves of strength you weren't aware of before.
- **Appreciation of Life**: Developing a heightened appreciation for life, even its most mundane aspects.
- **Relationships**: Experiencing deeper and more meaningful relationships with others.
- **New Possibilities**: Seeing new paths and opportunities that weren't apparent before.
- **Spiritual Development**: Deepening spiritual beliefs or discovering new spiritual understandings.

Integrating these elements of growth into your life requires patience and self-reflection. The process unfolds differently for everyone, influenced by their unique experiences, coping mechanisms, and support systems.

Role of Goals and Values

Aligning your actions with your core values and setting new goals is pivotal in finding purpose after loss. This alignment acts as a compass, guiding your steps as you navigate through grief toward a future that, while different from what you might have envisioned, is rich with potential and meaning.

- **Identify Your Values**: Take time to reflect on what truly matters to you. What principles do you want to guide your life?
- **Set Purpose-Driven Goals**: Based on your values, set meaningful goals. These could relate to personal growth, helping others, or pursuing interests that bring you joy.
- **Small Steps**: Break down your goals into manageable steps. Celebrate each milestone, no matter how small, as a testament to your resilience and forward movement.

Stories of Transformation

The power of personal stories to illuminate the path through grief cannot be overstated. These narratives serve as beacons, reminding us that renewal is possible and that loss while shaping us, does not define us.

- **Elena's Journey**: After losing her partner, Elena channeled her grief into advocacy, becoming a vocal supporter of heart health. Her loss led to a newfound purpose: ensuring others have the resources and knowledge to prevent similar tragedies.
- **Marcus' Rediscovery**: Marcus turned the pain of his career-ending injury into an opportunity to rediscover his love for art, a passion he had set aside. His artwork, deeply influenced by his journey through loss and recovery, comforts others facing their trials.
- **A Community's Resilience**: A small town devastated by a natural disaster came together to rebuild not just its homes but also its community spirit. Their collective effort sparked initiatives focusing on sustainability and community support, transforming tragedy into a legacy of strength and unity.

These stories, each with distinct features, share a common thread: the human spirit's ability to adapt, grow, and find new meaning in the face of loss. They remind us that, while the scars of loss may never entirely disappear, they mark us not as victims but survivors, capable of creating a narrative of resilience and hope.

In the wake of loss, discovering purpose is a deeply personal and universally meaningful endeavor. It involves reflecting on our experiences, uncovering new insights, and gradually redefining our place in the world. By reframing our understanding of loss, embracing growth after trauma, staying true to our values, and drawing inspiration from tales of change, we can thread our life events into a story beyond mere survival—it becomes a narrative of perseverance. This process does not erase the pain of loss but integrates it into a larger narrative of resilience and continual personal growth.

2.8 Nurturing Hope: The Seed of Resilience

In the landscape of our mind, hope shines as a guiding light, casting its brilliance through the shadows of despair. Hope is the belief in the possibility of positive outcomes amidst life's challenges, a crucial element for sustained motivation and resilience.

Defining Hope

Psychologists conceptualize hope as comprising two main components: the will to achieve one's goals (agency) and the pathways to reach those goals (pathways thinking). Hope is a dynamic mental state, contrasting with passive wishing, as it actively engages the individual in strategizing and pursuing objectives, even in the face of obstacles. This understanding of hope highlights its role not just as an emotion but as a cognitive process, enabling individuals to envision a future where their desires are fulfilled despite current adversities.

Hope as a Motivational Force

The power of hope lies in its ability to propel us forward, even when the odds seem stacked against us. It is a motivational force, igniting the drive to pursue our goals and persist through challenges. Hope fosters a proactive attitude, encouraging us to seek solutions and alternatives rather than succumbing to resignation.

For instance, consider the process of recovery from illness. Hope motivates individuals to adhere to treatment plans, maintain a positive outlook, and actively participate in their healing journey, even when progress seems slow. This active engagement with hope influences psychological well-being and can have tangible effects on physical health outcomes.

Cultivating Hope in Daily Life

You can nurture hope by integrating simple yet impactful actions into your everyday life:

- **Setting Achievable Goals**: Start by setting small, attainable goals. Achieving these can boost your confidence, creating a positive feedback loop that reinforces your sense of hope.
- **Visualizing Success**: Spend time visualizing and achieving your goals. This mental rehearsal can increase your belief in the possibility of success, fueling hope.
- **Building a Supportive Network**: Connect with individuals who share your aspirations and encourage your efforts. This community can be a source of

inspiration, advice, and encouragement, bolstering your hope.
- **Seeking Inspiration**: Immerse yourself in tales of resilience and victory, be it within literature, movies, or heartfelt discussions. These stories can reignite hope within you, serving as poignant reminders of life's joys and your inherent capacity to conquer challenges and adversity. Embracing such narratives can rejuvenate your belief in endless possibilities, rekindling a sense of purpose and revitalizing your hope for the future, guiding you away from suicidality and thoughts of despair toward a life filled with hope, meaning, and triumph.

The Impact of Hope on Mental Health

Research consistently demonstrates a strong correlation between hope and mental well-being. High levels of hope are associated with lower incidences of depression, anxiety, and stress. It serves as a buffer, protecting against the psychological toll of adverse life events and stressors.

A study published in *The Journal of Positive Psychology* examined the role of hope in coping with life challenges. The findings revealed that individuals with higher levels of hope exhibited greater emotional well-being and reported feeling more equipped to handle their difficulties. This research underscores hope's profound impact as a psychological asset in navigating life's ups and downs and as a foundational element for building and sustaining resilience.

Incorporating the practice of nurturing hope into our daily lives stands as a testament to our capacity for growth, adaptation, and resilience. By defining hope, understanding its role as a motivational force, actively cultivating it, and acknowledging its positive effects on our mental health, we equip ourselves with a powerful tool for navigating the complexities of life.

2.9 Creative Expression as a Pathway Out of Darkness

Creative expression is vital in navigating moments of darkness, providing solace, articulating emotions, and fostering healing and resilience. This unique form of expression navigates beyond the limitations of conventional language and offers a profound means of articulating and processing feelings that might otherwise remain buried.

Art as Therapy

The therapeutic benefits of engaging in creative activities are well-documented, revealing art's capacity to heal and transform. When words fail to capture the depth of our emotions, creating—be it through painting, writing, music, or dance—provides an alternative language. This non-verbal expression allows for externalizing internal experiences, fostering insight, catharsis, and emotional release. Notably, the focus here is not on the aesthetic outcome but on the creation process itself. Engaging in art as therapy is about letting the mind wander, and the heart speaks, using the canvas, the page, or the melody as receptacles for the complexities of the human experience.

Expression Beyond Words

There are moments when words alone may fall short or lack the intricate means required to articulate our deepest emotions fully. Creative expression taps into our psyche's non-linear, non-rational aspects, allowing the subconscious to surface. This process can unveil hidden emotions, clarify confusion, and offer new perspectives on old pains. For many, it feels like unlocking a door to a room long closed, where the light of awareness can now enter and illuminate what was previously obscured.

To begin exploring this expressive path:

- Allow yourself to experiment without judgment. The goal is not to create a masterpiece but to connect with your inner world.
- Use prompts if you find yourself facing a blank canvas or page. A single word, a color, or a piece of music can spark the creative process.
- Reflect on your creations. After you've expressed yourself, spend time contemplating your work. What emotions does it evoke? What thoughts arise?

Starting a Creative Practice

The prospect of starting can be daunting for those new to creative expression. The process may seem silly to some folks or unnatural or unfamiliar. However, the journey into art as a therapy requires no prior experience or skill—only openness and the willingness to explore. Here are a few steps to help you begin:

- Choose a medium that appeals to you. Whether you draw, journal, sculpt, or play an instrument, select a form of expression that resonates with you.
- Create a dedicated space. Having a specific area where you can engage in your creative practice can help foster a routine and signal to your mind that it's time to focus inwardly.

- Set aside regular time. Consistency is key. Even just a few minutes a day can be immensely beneficial in developing your practice and reaping its therapeutic rewards.

Case Studies of Creative Healing

The stories of those who have found solace and healing through creative expression are as varied as the individuals, yet each shares a common transformation thread.

- **Maya's Journey Through Grief**: After a colleague of mine, Maya, lost a loved one, she found herself unable to articulate her grief verbally. After the subsequent onset of depression and months of daily emotional struggles, her best friend reached out, offering her support. She recommended that they discover alternative ways or methods for her to articulate and deal with her feelings. She began to process her emotions through painting, and the colors and strokes on the canvas mirrored the turbulence within. Over time, her art became a visual diary of her healing process, each marking a step forward in her journey through grief.
- **Eli's Battle With Anxiety**: A few months back, I encountered a patient, whom I'll refer to as "Eli," at an outpatient clinic. He opened up to me about a new method he had been using to help combat his frequent anxiety and find healing. Eli found that writing poetry served as a lifeline in coping with his anxiety, a discovery that took him by surprise as he had never shown much interest in poetry before this chapter of his life. The rhythmic structure and the need to find the right word provided a focus that quieted his racing thoughts. Through poetry, he

could express fears and hopes that he had struggled to share verbally, finding relief and understanding.
- **Emma's Dance of Liberation**: A cherished friend of our family has a young adult daughter, whom I'll call Emma, who became part of their lives through adoption at the age of 10. Before joining their family, Emma faced profound hardships, including the loss of a sibling and parent in a traumatic accident, alongside the uncertainties and pressures of navigating the foster care system in search of a secure home.

Following these events, Emma continued to struggle with ongoing depression and anxiety, frequently feeling a profound sense of detachment from her body and emotions. Nonetheless, her engagement with dance initiated a deep journey of self-discovery for Emma. The expressive power of movement gave her an outlet to voice the silent struggles that weighed her down, seamlessly connecting her internal conflicts and her external world. With every movement in dance, she began to uncover and piece together fragments of her identity, crafting a resilient and healing mosaic over time.

These stories emphasize the incredible power of creative expression to tackle the challenges of mental health and emotional healing. They highlight that each of us harbors a rich source of creativity, which can serve as a foundation for comfort, insight, and transformation. Art becomes a way to voice unspoken emotions, shape intangible thoughts, and illuminate a pathway from darkness to understanding and acceptance.

THREE

Forging Connections for Healing

I magine standing at a crossroads, unsure of which path to take. Each direction promises a different landscape and unique challenges and rewards. This moment, filled with potential and uncertainty, mirrors the process of seeking out mental health support. You know you need assistance, but many options can feel overwhelming. Yet, it's this very act of reaching out, of mapping the terrain of support available, that marks the first step toward healing.

3.1 Identifying and Accessing Support Systems

Mapping Local and Online Resources

The landscape of mental health resources is vast, encompassing everything from local support groups and therapists to online forums and mobile apps. Finding the right resources involves a bit of detective work. Start by listing what you're looking for in a support system—do you prefer face-to-face interactions or the anonymity of online support? Are you seeking professional therapy, or would a peer support group better suit your needs?

- **Local Resources**: Community centers, hospitals, and mental health clinics often host support groups and workshops. Libraries and bulletin boards can also be treasure troves of information on local therapists and counselors.
- **Online Resources**: Websites like Psychology Today offer directories of therapists, while platforms such as Meetup can connect you with local and virtual support groups. Don't overlook apps geared toward mental wellness, which can provide tools for managing anxiety, depression, and stress.

Evaluating the Right Fit

Only some therapists or support groups will be the right match for your unique needs. When considering your options, reflect on the following criteria to ensure a good fit:

- **Specialization**: Does the professional or group specialize in addressing your specific challenges or concerns?
- **Approach**: Consider the therapeutic or support approach. Do you prefer structured therapy methods, or are you looking for a more open-ended discussion group?
- **Compatibility**: Ask yourself if you felt heard and understood after attending a session or meeting. Trust your gut feeling about whether this environment would be supportive for you.

Overcoming Barriers to Access

Several hurdles can stand in the way of accessing support, from logistical challenges like transportation and scheduling to emotional barriers such as fear of stigma. Here are strategies to navigate these obstacles:

- **Logistical Challenges**: Many therapists offer virtual sessions, which can eliminate transportation issues. Flexible scheduling, including evening and weekend appointments, can help fit therapy into a busy life.
- **Financial Concerns**: Inquire about sliding scale fees or insurance coverage. Some support groups and resources are free, making them accessible regardless of financial situation.
- **Emotional Hurdles**: Reaching out for help can be daunting. Remember, seeking support is a sign of strength.

Start small—perhaps by confiding in a trusted friend about your search for support or attending an online support group where you can remain anonymous until you feel more comfortable.

The Role of Advocacy in Accessing Support

Advocating for yourself or a loved one is sometimes necessary to navigate the mental health system effectively. This might mean requesting a referral from your general practitioner, requesting information on therapists' specializations, or even advocating for mental health coverage with your insurance provider. Community advocacy can also play a role, such as campaigning for more accessible mental health services or organizing community support networks.

- **Self-Advocacy Tips**: Prepare questions in advance for healthcare providers, and don't hesitate to follow up for more information or clarification. Keep a record of your interactions and any vital information you receive.
- **Community Advocacy Ideas**: Join or form a local mental health advocacy group. These groups can work together to host informational events, petition for changes in local mental health policies, or provide a collective voice in support of community mental health needs.

Embarking on the quest for the ideal support system is a deeply personal journey that reflects each person's unique experiences and needs. Identifying available resources, assessing them against individual preferences and requirements, navigating potential hindrances, and actively participating in self- and community advocacy are essential steps in this voyage. Such a journey, demanding patience and persistence, fosters healing and builds resilience.

3.2 The Importance of Peer Support Groups in Healing

Stepping into a space through a screen or in person, where you find reflections of your journey in those around you, is profoundly transformative. Such experiences capture the essence of peer support groups—settings grounded in empathy, shared understanding, and the collective wisdom critical for healing. In these gatherings, stories and struggles are heard and deeply felt, providing a unique form of solace and a powerful sense of belonging.

Benefits of Peer Support

Peer support groups offer a unique blend of camaraderie and mutual understanding that can sometimes elude formal therapy settings. These groups serve as a sanctuary where shared experiences forge connections, diminish the sting of isolation, and nurture a comforting sense of community. Within this space, individuals receive support and discover role models, gaining insights into peers' varied strategies to surmount their challenges. This dynamic can significantly boost motivation, as observing peers navigate hurdles successfully instills tangible hope and inspiration.

- Members exchange knowledge and practical advice born from lived experience.
- The group provides a safe space to share without fear of judgment, promoting emotional release.
- Witnessing the resilience of others in the group can be incredibly empowering.

Finding the Right Group

Locating a peer support group that aligns with your distinct experiences and aspirations requires thoughtful self-reflection and diligent research. Consider what you hope to achieve – learning new ways to cope, seeking a secure environment for self-expression, or finding camaraderie among peers. A precise grasp of your aims equips you to explore your options more effectively.

- Local mental health organizations or hospitals often have lists of active groups.
- Online platforms dedicated to mental health, where many support groups advertise their meetings.
- Social media networks, where hashtags related to specific mental health challenges can lead you to relevant groups.

Finding where you feel most at home might take several sessions with different groups.

Online vs. In-Person Groups

The decision between online and in-person support groups hinges on personal preference and circumstances. Each format offers distinct advantages and challenges:

Online Groups:

- **Pros**: They are accessible from anywhere, offering convenience and a degree of anonymity that can encourage openness. They also support those needing more local options due to geographic or mobility limitations.

- **Cons**: The lack of physical presence can sometimes make it harder to form deep connections. Technical issues or platform limitations can also hinder communication.

In-Person Groups:

- **Pros**: The physical presence of others can enhance feelings of connection and support. Non-verbal cues and body language add depth to communication, making empathy and understanding more palpable.
- **Cons**: Logistics such as transportation and scheduling can be barriers. Some might also feel apprehensive about sharing in a face-to-face setting.

Weighing these factors against your needs and comfort level will help guide your choice.

Starting Your Own Group

If existing groups don't meet your needs or if you're motivated to create a space for a specific subset of peers, starting your own group is a viable option. Here's a simplified roadmap:

1. **Define the Purpose and Scope**: Clearly outline the group's focus, whether it's a specific mental health condition, a shared life experience, or a general support space. This clarity will guide all subsequent decisions.
2. **Choose a Format**: Consider whether the group will meet online or in person, and consider the needs and preferences of potential members.
3. **Set Guidelines**: Establish clear rules regarding confidentiality, communication styles, and meeting structure to ensure a safe and supportive environment.

4. **Promote Your Group**: To reach potential members, use social media, community bulletin boards, and partnerships with local mental health organizations.
5. **Facilitate Meetings**: Prepare topics or questions to guide discussion, especially in the early meetings. Over time, the group may evolve to have a more fluid structure based on members' needs.
6. **Seek Feedback**: Regularly check in with group members to discuss their experiences and identify improvements to meet their goals.

Initiating and maintaining a support group requires commitment, effort, and patience. Nevertheless, developing a supportive community through these endeavors creates a healing and empowering environment for everyone involved. The essence of peer support groups lies in the profound impact of sharing and understanding similar experiences. These groups provide support and cultivate a sense of belonging, creating a community where individual stories are acknowledged and appreciated. Whether you are in search of a group that aligns with your specific needs or you are driven to establish a new gathering space for others, embarking on the path of peer support groups opens up a distinctive route to resilience and healing, underscoring the importance of connection and mutual support in the journey towards recovery.

3.3 Role of Family Dynamics in Suicide Prevention

The complex network of relationships within a family significantly influences its members' emotional and mental health. These connections can be crucial support systems, offering understanding and comfort in challenging times. However, when these relationships are strained, they can intensify feelings of loneliness and despair. Thus, acknowledging and enhancing the role of family dynamics is essential in suicide prevention efforts.

Understanding Family Influence

Family dynamics significantly impact mental health, shaping perspectives, coping mechanisms, and resilience to adversity. In suicide prevention, families play a critical role, not only providing support but actively engaging in recognizing distress signals and promoting an environment where mental health discussions are normalized.

- Insight into individual struggles becomes more transparent when viewed through familial interactions.
- Positive reinforcement from family members can significantly boost one's self-esteem and sense of belonging, crucial elements in combatting feelings of worthlessness or isolation often associated with suicidal ideation.

Improving Communication Within the Family

Open and sincere dialogue is foundational to fostering a supportive environment within families. It establishes a bedrock of trust, creating a safe space for individuals to share their vulnerabilities and seek assistance. To augment family communication, families should actively listen, communicate with empathy, and cultivate an environment that encourages the free expression of emotions without judgment or backlash.

- **Active Listening**: Prioritize understanding the speaker's perspective over formulating a response. Acknowledge feelings and offer non-verbal cues of engagement.

- **Emotional Vocabulary**: Cultivate a rich emotional vocabulary within the family, allowing for precise articulation of feelings and experiences. This practice demystifies emotions, making them easier to discuss and address.
- **Regular Check-ins**: Establish a routine of regular family meetings or one-on-one conversations dedicated to sharing feelings, experiences, and concerns. This routine reinforces the notion that each member's mental wellness is paramount.

Supporting a Family Member in Crisis

When a family member is facing suicidal thoughts, it plunges the whole family into unknown territory, filled with anxiety, perplexity, and an intense wish to be supportive. In these critical times, it's essential to offer support that respects the individual's independence while ensuring they feel cared for and understood.

- **Educate Yourselves**: Equip yourselves with knowledge about suicide prevention, understanding both the warning signs and how to respond effectively.
- **Professional Help**: Encourage seeking professional help while offering to assist in the process, whether by researching therapists, making appointments, or providing transportation.
- **Unconditional Support**: Affirm your unconditional love and support. Ensure the individual knows their worth to the family and that their struggles do not diminish their value or the love you hold for them.

Family Therapy as a Resource

Family therapy is a valuable approach to tackling and mitigating dysfunctional family dynamics that might exacerbate an individual's distress. This method enhances communication, fosters mutual understanding, and promotes healing across the family spectrum. Its goal is to address and settle conflicts, strengthen familial bonds, and cultivate a nurturing home atmosphere that supports mental well-being.

- **Identifying Patterns**: A trained therapist can help identify recurring patterns of behavior or communication that may contribute to stress or conflict within the family.
- **Developing Strategies**: Through therapy, families can create new strategies for handling disagreements, supporting one another, and fostering a positive home environment.
- **Healing Together**: Family therapy creates a space for collective healing, acknowledging that each member contributes to the family's overall health and that together, they can forge a more robust, supportive unit.

The critical role of family dynamics in suicide prevention is undeniable. We can enact meaningful transformations by recognizing the powerful impact these relationships hold and taking active steps to enhance communication, offer empathetic support during crises, and engage in family therapy. These measures cultivate environments of support and understanding, thereby enhancing resilience.

3.4 How to Offer Support Without Offering Solutions

Extending support to someone in distress often propels us toward attempting to solve their issues. This well-meaning impulse, however, frequently overlooks the individual's actual needs: to be listened to, comprehended, and affirmed. Developing the ability to offer support without rushing to provide solutions is a nuanced but deeply impactful skill, fostering an environment where individuals feel empowered to confront their own challenges.

Listening with Empathy

At the heart of meaningful support is listening—not just hearing the words spoken but genuinely understanding the emotions and experiences behind them. Empathetic listening requires immersing oneself in the viewpoint of the other, putting aside personal biases and preconceived solutions. It's about crafting an environment where individuals feel genuinely acknowledged and understood, validating their emotions as real and vital.

- **Reflect**: Sometimes, simply mirroring back what you've heard can be powerful. Phrases like, "It sounds like you're feeling..." help the person feel understood.
- **Non-Verbal Cues**: Your body language speaks volumes. Maintain eye contact, nod in understanding, and lean slightly to convey your full engagement and empathy.

Avoiding the Fix-It Trap

In our society, being a problem-solver is often highly esteemed. Yet, in providing emotional support, this mindset can unintentionally diminish the individual's feelings and experiences. The compulsion to offer immediate solutions, rooted in a wish to ease both their discomfort and our own, can result in the individual feeling overlooked and their emotional state invalidated. Focusing on being present for them in their moment of need is crucial, as it helps suppress the impulse to fix their problems swiftly.

- **Pause Before Responding**: Consider whether advice is genuinely what the person is seeking or if they need a compassionate ear.
- **Ask Permission**: If you feel compelled to offer advice, you could first ask, "Would you like to hear some thoughts or ideas, or would you prefer just to talk it out?"

Validating Feelings

Validation is recognizing and accepting another person's feelings, thoughts, and experiences as understandable and legitimate. In the context of supporting someone with suicidal ideation, validation becomes a lifeline, a message that their feelings matter and they are not alone in their pain. It's about affirming the complexity and depth of their emotions without judgment or an immediate push toward resolution.

- **Avoid Minimizing Language**: Phrases like "It could be worse" or "You should just try to be positive" can feel dismissive. Instead, use validating language such as, "That sounds incredibly hard" or "I can see why you'd feel that way."
- **Acknowledge Their Strength**: Recognizing the strength to share vulnerable feelings can be validating. Remind them of their courage in opening up.

Empowering Individuals to Seek Solutions

Empowerment in this context means encouraging individuals to discover and pursue their own solutions, fostering a sense of autonomy and control over their situation. This approach acknowledges that the person is the expert on their own life and can navigate their path to healing with support rather than directives from others.

- **Encourage Reflection**: Prompt them to consider their own needs and feelings by asking open-ended questions like, "What do you feel you need most right now?" or "What has helped you in the past when you've felt this way?"
- **Highlight Their Agency**: Remind them of their ability to choose for their well-being, even in small ways. This could be as simple as engaging in a comforting activity or reaching out to a professional for help.
- **Offer Resources, Not Prescriptions**: If they are open to it, provide information on resources—therapists, hotlines, support groups—without pushing them towards any single option. Frame it as, "Here are some options you might consider," leaving the choice firmly in their hands.

In supporting someone through the dark tunnels of their experience, the most profound gift we can offer is not solutions but presence, empathy, and validation. By engaging in empathetic listening, refraining from rushing to provide solutions, validating the emotions of others, and fostering self-directed problem-solving, we create a supportive atmosphere conducive to recovery. This approach strengthens a connection based on mutual respect and understanding, empowering the person to embark on their own path toward resilience and renewal.

3.5 Creating Safe Spaces for Open Conversations

Establishing environments that encourage individuals to express their deepest emotions and thoughts openly is crucial for fostering mental well-being. Physical and virtual environments evolve beyond simple places to be pillars of empathy, trust, and understanding. They lay the groundwork for nurturing frank and candid conversations about mental health and suicide prevention.

Principles of Safe Space Creation

At the core of creating a safe environment lie steadfast principles that prioritize the essence of open dialogue. Respect takes precedence, acknowledging and appreciating each individual's unique story and experiences and honoring their courage in sharing. Equally crucial is a pledge to refrain from passing judgment, ensuring that every narrative is met with openness and compassion, free from bias. Inclusivity is fundamental, shaping an atmosphere where people from diverse backgrounds feel acknowledged and valued. Lastly, empathy plays a vital role in fostering deep emotional connections that nurture genuine understanding and connection.

- **Respect**: Acknowledge each person's experiences and feelings as valid and significant, affirming their worth.
- **Non-Judgment**: Approach each conversation with an open mind, suspending any preconceived notions or biases.
- **Inclusivity**: Ensure that the space welcomes all individuals, embracing a diversity of experiences and perspectives.
- **Empathy**: Strive to deeply understand and connect with others' emotions, offering compassion and solidarity.

Role of Confidentiality

Confidentiality serves as the foundation for trust in a secure environment. It ensures that conversations within these safe boundaries stay confidential, creating an atmosphere of safety and transparency. This trust empowers individuals to share their innermost thoughts, challenges, and aspirations, knowing their disclosures will be kept secure. Setting clear confidentiality guidelines is crucial, ensuring everyone comprehends and upholds this essential aspect of the safe space.

- **Explicit Assurance**: At the beginning of every session or meeting, reiterate the importance of confidentiality and the expectation that all shared information remains within the group.
- **Establish Boundaries**: Clearly define what information can be shared outside the group and what must remain confidential, ensuring all members are on the same page.
- **Build Trust**: Consistently uphold confidentiality to build trust over time, reinforcing the safe space's integrity and members' security.

Facilitating Supportive Conversations

Guiding supportive and constructive conversations requires a delicate balance, ensuring that every individual feels heard and valued. Begin by setting a positive tone, one that encourages openness and honesty. Actively listen, offering your full attention to the speaker, and respond with empathy and understanding. Use open-ended questions to delve deeper into the person's experiences, allowing them to explore their feelings and thoughts more fully.

- **Active Listening**: Give speakers undivided attention, acknowledging their words with nods or verbal affirmations.
- **Empathetic Responses**: Respond with phrases that express understanding and compassion, such as "That sounds incredibly challenging" or "I can only imagine how that must feel."
- **Open-Ended Questions**: Encourage deeper reflection with questions like "How did that make you feel?" or "What do you think you need most right now?"

Addressing and Preventing Stigma

The stigma surrounding mental health and suicide poses a significant obstacle to open dialogues, reinforcing misconceptions and suppressing those seeking help. Combatting and eradicating stigma within safe settings entails directly confronting these falsehoods and cultivating an atmosphere of inclusivity and empathy. Share accurate knowledge about mental health and suicide to debunk misconceptions and showcase narratives of resilience and optimism to counter harmful stereotypes. Foster an environment where mental health conversations are approached with the same level of openness and gravity as physical health, making these discussions commonplace.

- **Challenge Misconceptions**: Correct false beliefs or stereotypes when they arise, providing factual information about mental health and suicide.
- **Share Stories of Hope**: Highlight narratives of recovery and resilience to offer hope and counteract stigma.
- **Normalize Mental Health Conversations**: Treat discussions about mental health as normal and necessary, akin to conversations about physical well-being.

Fostering environments conducive to open discussions on mental health and suicide prevention is a continuous and evolving endeavor. It necessitates a foundation of respect, stringent confidentiality, active, empathetic engagement, and a vigilant approach toward dismantling stigma. Through our commitment to these guiding principles, we lay the foundation for spaces that recognize and understand each individual and empower them to share their stories with courage and confidence.

3.6 The Power of Community Programs in Suicide Prevention

Community programs play a pivotal role in weaving the fabric of support necessary for effective suicide prevention. These initiatives stand as testaments to what can be achieved when individuals unite with a common goal: to save lives and foster an environment where mental well-being is prioritized. They are not just programs but lifelines that reach the depths of despair, offering hope and practical assistance.

Examples of Effective Programs

Several community-based suicide prevention programs have showcased remarkable results, becoming beacons of hope and models for replication. One notable example is the Gatekeeper training program, which equips community members with the skills to identify individuals at risk of suicide and guide them toward help. Schools, workplaces, and religious communities have successfully implemented this program, increasing awareness and early intervention.

Another innovative approach is the Crisis Text Line, a free, 24/7 text-based service that provides immediate support to individuals in crisis. By offering anonymity and accessibility, this service breaks down barriers to seeking help, especially among younger populations who may prefer texting over talking.

Community resilience models focus on strengthening the collective ability of a community to support individuals facing mental health challenges. These models emphasize building a network of resources, including accessible mental health services, supportive social environments, and public awareness campaigns that collectively enhance the community's capacity to prevent suicides.

Engaging Community Members

The success of community programs hinges on the active engagement of community members. Strategies to foster this engagement include:

- **Awareness Campaigns**: Implementing targeted campaigns that educate the community about suicide risk factors, warning signs, and how to offer support can demystify the topic and encourage proactive involvement.
- **Volunteer Opportunities**: Offering varied volunteer roles within suicide prevention initiatives allows community members to contribute in ways that align with their skills and comfort levels, from facilitating support groups to assisting in fundraising efforts.
- **Community Workshops**: Hosting workshops on mental health, stress management, and suicide prevention provides valuable education and skills training, empowering community members to support each other.

Training Community Leaders

Community leaders, including educators, faith leaders, and local officials, hold influential positions that can significantly impact suicide prevention efforts. By receiving specialized training in suicide prevention, these leaders can:

- Recognize early signs of mental distress and suicidal ideation among community members.
- Provide immediate support and referral to professional help.
- Use their platforms to advocate for mental health awareness and the destigmatization of seeking help.

Faith leaders, in particular, can bridge the gap between spiritual support and mental health resources, offering guidance that resonates with their communities' values and beliefs. Training for these leaders focuses on compassionate listening, ethical considerations, and collaboration with mental health professionals.

Evaluating Program Impact

Assessing the impact of community programs is crucial for understanding their effectiveness and areas for improvement. Evaluation methods include:

- **Surveys and Feedback**: Collecting feedback from program participants and community members can provide insights into the program's reach and perceived value. Surveys can assess changes in knowledge, attitudes, and behaviors regarding suicide prevention.
- **Data Analysis**: Monitoring local suicide rates, instances of crisis interventions, and utilization of mental health

services can offer quantifiable measures of a program's impact. Comparing these metrics before and after the implementation of community programs can highlight changes in trends.
- **Qualitative Stories**: Gathering personal stories and testimonials from individuals the program has directly impacted adds depth to quantitative data, illustrating the program's effect on individual lives.

This evaluation process measures success and identifies gaps in services or areas where the community's needs have evolved, guiding future enhancements to the program.

In summary, the power of community programs in suicide prevention lies in their ability to unite individuals around a shared purpose, equip them with the knowledge and skills to support one another, and create an environment where mental health is openly discussed and valued. Through effective implementation, active community engagement, specialized training for leaders, and rigorous evaluation, these programs can significantly reduce the incidence of suicide and build a foundation of resilience and hope within communities.

3.7 Technology and Apps: Modern Tools for Connection

In today's digital age, technology has seamlessly woven into the fabric of our daily lives, offering unprecedented access to information, resources, and, importantly, support for mental health. The advent of apps and online platforms has revolutionized how we connect with therapeutic resources, providing tools that complement traditional methods of mental health care. This section explores the digital frontier of mental health support, evaluating the effectiveness and safety of these modern tools and understanding their place in the broader spectrum of mental wellness strategies.

Digital Mental Health Resources

The digital landscape is rich with resources designed to support mental health. From mindfulness apps that guide users through meditation exercises to platforms offering cognitive behavioral therapy techniques, these tools cater to a wide range of needs. Mobile applications like Headspace and Calm focus on stress reduction and mindfulness, while others, such as Talkspace and BetterHelp, connect users with licensed therapists for virtual counseling sessions. Additionally, mood-tracking apps provide users with the means to monitor their emotional states over time, offering insights that can be invaluable in managing conditions like anxiety and depression.

- **Variety**: The range of apps covers various aspects of mental health, including mindfulness, therapy, mood tracking, and stress management.
- **Accessibility**: Digital tools are accessible to anyone with a smartphone or internet access, breaking down barriers related to geography or mobility.
- **Anonymity**: These platforms can offer privacy and anonymity for those hesitant to seek face-to-face counseling.

Evaluating Digital Tools

While the abundance of digital mental health tools is a boon, assessing their effectiveness and safety is crucial. Not all apps and platforms are created equal, and the lack of regulation in the digital health space can lead to variability in quality. When evaluating these tools, consider:

- **Credibility**: Look for apps developed or endorsed by mental health professionals or reputable organizations.
- **Privacy**: Understand how your data is stored and used. Reputable apps will have clear, accessible privacy policies detailing data handling practices.
- **User Reviews and Feedback**: While subjective, user experiences can offer insights into the app's usability and effectiveness.
- **Evidence-based**: People prefer tools that approach stress reduction using scientifically validated methods, such as CBT or mindfulness.

The Role of Teletherapy

Teletherapy, providing therapy services via video conferencing, email, or messaging, has become vital to mental health care. This method of delivering therapy offers flexibility and convenience, making mental health support more accessible to those with busy schedules, physical disabilities, or those living in remote areas.

- **Benefits**: Eliminates travel time, offers scheduling flexibility, and can make therapy more accessible financially and logistically.
- **Limitations**: It may only be suitable for some types of therapy or all clients, especially those who require more intensive, hands-on interventions or who lack a private, secure space for sessions.

When considering teletherapy, it is essential to work with a therapist experienced in delivering services remotely and using secure, confidential platforms designed for healthcare communications.

Online Communities and Forums

Online communities and forums dedicated to mental health provide spaces where individuals can share experiences, offer support, and find a sense of belonging among peers facing similar challenges. Websites like 7 Cups or forums on platforms like Reddit allow users to connect anonymously, share their stories, and receive support from a global community.

- **Peer Support**: These platforms often facilitate peer-to-peer support, allowing individuals to give and receive advice, share coping strategies, and encourage.
- **Moderation and Safety**: Well-moderated forums have guidelines and moderators to ensure discussions remain respectful, supportive, and safe.
- **Limitations**: While these communities can offer significant support, it's important to remember that peer advice is not a substitute for professional mental health care. Users should be cautious about sharing personal information and critical of the advice they receive.

Integrating technology into mental health support opens new avenues for individuals to connect with resources, professionals, and peers. Whether through apps that guide mindfulness practices, platforms that facilitate virtual therapy sessions, or online communities offering peer support, these digital tools expand the horizons of mental health care. However, evaluating these resources for credibility, privacy, and evidence-based approaches is crucial to ensure they are beneficial supplements to traditional mental health treatments. As we navigate this digital landscape, the potential to harness technology to support mental wellness has never been more significant, offering hope and assistance at the touch of a button or the click of a mouse.

3.8 Educators as Pillars of Support: A Guide for Schools

In the nurturing halls of education, where young minds blossom and grow, lies an often untapped wellspring of support for mental health. Schools, with their daily access to youth, are uniquely positioned to be frontline defenders in the battle against the shadows of anxiety, depression, and suicidal ideation. Here, we navigate through the corridors of creating a school environment that, brick by brick, builds a sanctuary of understanding, support, and proactive care for its students.

Implementing School-Based Mental Health Programs

Creating an effective school-based mental health program demands a multifaceted approach, integrating various components to address the broad spectrum of student needs. It starts with developing a curriculum that includes mental health education, teaching students about emotional wellness, coping strategies, and seeking help. Embedding mental health into the broader educational framework demystifies the topic, encouraging open dialogue and early intervention.

- **Preventative Workshops and Seminars**: Facilitate regular events focused on stress management, emotional literacy, and healthy relationships to equip students with the necessary tools before crises arise.

- **Peer Support Systems**: Train select students as peer mentors, offering support layers and creating a student-led network of empathy and understanding.
- **Access to Mental Health Professionals**: Ensure students have easy access to on-site psychologists or counselors who can provide immediate support and intervention.

Training Teachers and Staff

Teachers and school staff are often the first to notice changes in a student's behavior that may indicate mental health struggles. Their training in identifying and responding to these signs is crucial.

- **Recognizing Warning Signs**: Equip educators with the knowledge to spot early indicators of mental distress, such as withdrawal, sudden changes in academic performance, or alterations in mood and behavior.
- **Intervention Techniques**: Teach staff how to approach and talk to students showing signs of distress, using empathetic communication to encourage them to share their experiences and feelings.
- **Referral Processes**: Clarify the steps educators should take if they believe a student needs professional help, including how to connect them with school mental health resources or external support services.

Creating a Supportive School Environment

The atmosphere of a school plays a critical role in promoting mental health. A culture that champions empathy, inclusivity, and compassion supports students in need and fosters an environment where everyone feels safe and valued.

- **Anti-Bullying Policies**: Implement and enforce robust anti-bullying measures to create a safe space where all students feel secure.
- **Mental Health Days**: Recognize mental health days for students, acknowledging the importance of mental well-being as equivalent to physical health.
- **Inclusivity Programs**: Develop programs that celebrate diversity and promote inclusivity, ensuring every student feels a sense of belonging and acceptance.

Engaging Parents and Caregivers

Parents and caregivers are vital in bolstering student mental health. Their engagement broadens the support network beyond school boundaries, ensuring a cohesive approach in practice and conversation to assist the student more effectively.

- **Information Sessions**: Host sessions for parents and caregivers on understanding mental health, recognizing signs of distress in their children, and effectively providing support at home.
- **Open Communication Channels**: Establish clear and open lines of communication between the school and home, allowing for the sharing of concerns and collaborative planning for the student's well-being.
- **Resource Sharing**: Provide parents with resources, including literature on mental health topics and information about external support services, to empower them with knowledge and options for seeking help in their local areas.

At the core of every educational institution is the potential to serve as a cornerstone of mental health support, fostering understanding and proactive care. Schools can evolve into nurturing spaces that promote academic growth and emotional and psychological resilience by adopting comprehensive mental health programs, educating teachers, and engaging parents and caregivers. This shift not only aids students but also enhances the broader school community, fostering a culture of empathy, resilience, and collective well-being that reaches beyond the confines of the classroom.

3.9 Workplace Mental Health: Building a Supportive Culture

In today's fast-paced world, the workplace is more than just a place for professional tasks; it's a central part of our lives where we spend considerable time. With its unique stresses and pressures, this environment significantly impacts our well-being. Recognizing this, employers play a vital role in creating a culture that acknowledges and actively supports mental health.

The Role of Employers in Supporting Mental Health

Employers must adopt a proactive approach to create a supportive workplace environment. To achieve this goal, employers should prioritize mental health, physical safety, and job performance. Doing so helps dismantle the stigma associated with mental health issues, encouraging employees to seek help without fear of reprisal or judgment. Regular mental health awareness sessions can educate both employees and management on recognizing signs of mental distress and understanding the importance of mental well-being. Such initiatives can transform the workplace into a space where mental health is openly discussed, fostering an atmosphere of understanding and support.

Implementing Mental Health Policies

Establishing a mentally healthy workplace begins with creating clear and comprehensive mental health policies. These policies are essential for detailing the support accessible to employees, explaining how employees can access this support, and clarifying the rights and responsibilities of everyone involved. Crucial elements of these policies could encompass:

- **Flexible Working Arrangements**: Offering varied work hours or the option to work from home can significantly reduce stress for employees with mental health issues.
- **Leave Policies**: Clearly defined leave policies for mental health purposes, distinguishing them from standard medical leave, can encourage employees to take time off when needed without fear of stigma.
- **Confidentiality Protocols**: Ensuring that discussions about mental health issues will be treated with strict confidentiality reassures employees that their privacy will be respected.
- **Employee Assistance Programs (EAPs)**: EAPs offer direct support for distressed employees by providing access to counseling services or therapy.

Resources for Employees

Beyond implementing policies, providing tangible resources is essential. Employers can offer a variety of supports tailored to meet diverse needs, ensuring employees have access to the help they require. These resources might include:

- **In-House Counseling Services**: On-site counselors or psychologists offer a convenient option for employees seeking help.
- **Online Support Platforms**: Subscriptions to digital mental health services or apps can provide employees with flexible support options.
- **Mental Health Days**: Dedicated mental health days encourage employees to take time off for self-care without dipping into their standard leave.
- **Training Sessions**: Workshops on stress management, resilience building, and healthy work-life balance equip employees with tools to manage their mental well-being.

Promoting Work-Life Balance

Supporting mental health in the workplace involves advocating for a healthy work-life balance. This balance is crucial for preventing burnout and ensuring employees can sustain their productivity without sacrificing their well-being. Employers can promote this balance by:

- **Setting Clear Expectations**: Clarify that long hours and constant availability differ from the success standards. Encourage employees to disconnect outside of work hours.
- **Modeling Behavior**: Leadership should exemplify work-life balance, visibly taking time off and refraining from sending work communications during evenings or weekends.
- **Encouraging Time Off**: Actively encourage employees to use their vacation days and take breaks throughout the day to recharge.

- **Providing Flexibility**: Where possible, offer flexible scheduling options, allowing employees to adapt their work hours to fit their personal lives and commitments.

Employers play a vital role in fostering workplace environments that support mental well-being through clear policies and resources and promoting work-life balance. By prioritizing mental health, organizations can enhance employee well-being, productivity, and loyalty. This approach acknowledges the connection between organizational and employee health, making mental well-being a central business priority.

3.10 Spiritual Communities: A Resource for Hope and Healing

Within every spiritual community, there is a rich reservoir of compassion, understanding, and shared strength. Rooted in common beliefs and values, these communities provide a unique refuge for individuals dealing with mental struggles, including thoughts of suicide. Here, spirituality and faith come together, weaving a supportive network that can uplift those in need and offer solace to troubled hearts.

The Role of Faith in Healing

Spirituality can serve as a vital anchor amid life's most challenging moments, with its profound connection to one's belief in life's purpose and meaning. Faith groups' rituals, prayers, and communal bonds can foster a sense of belonging and peace. These elements can help individuals facing suicidal thoughts see the value in life and a glimmer of hope during dark times. Shared faith experiences alleviate isolation and reinforce individuals' sense of worth and the available support during challenges. Faith communities are designed to be safe havens of love and acceptance, with spiritual teachings emphasizing compassion, resilience, and the inherent value of every life, providing powerful antidotes to feelings of hopelessness and inadequacy linked to suicidal ideation.

Engaging Faith Leaders

Faith leaders play a vital role as trusted figures in their communities, especially during crises. Their contribution to suicide prevention and mental health support is invaluable. By familiarizing themselves with signs of mental distress and available resources, leaders can help their congregations access healing and professional assistance.

Tailored training programs for faith leaders bridge the gap between spiritual support and mental health awareness, providing the tools to identify those in need, offer initial help, and refer individuals to mental health professionals. Addressing mental health openly in sermons and communal gatherings also helps destigmatize these issues, encouraging more people to seek help.

Spiritual Practices as Support

Spiritual rituals and practices provide deep comfort and stability for those dealing with mental health challenges. Engaging in meditation, prayer, and religious ceremonies can bring calm, clarity, and a sense of connection to something larger than oneself. These activities also offer a structured approach to managing anxiety, grief, and despair, allowing individuals to navigate their emotions, discover purpose, and build resilience.

- **Meditative Practices**: Techniques like mindfulness meditation or prayerful contemplation can help quiet the mind and foster a sense of inner peace.

- **Community Worship**: Participating in communal worship offers a sense of belonging and an opportunity to experience collective support and affirmation.
- **Sacred Texts and Teachings**: Many find comfort and guidance in the stories, parables, and teachings within the holy texts or scriptures of their faith, which can offer perspectives on suffering, resilience, and the value of life.

Building Bridges Between Faith and Mental Health Services

When spiritual communities and mental health professionals collaborate, they create a holistic support system for individuals' spiritual and psychological well-being. Partnering with local mental health practitioners, clinics, and support groups allows faith communities to broaden their support, building a comprehensive care network for those in need.

Strategies for fostering these collaborations include:

- Hosting joint workshops and seminars that address mental health from both spiritual and clinical perspectives.
- Establish referral networks that faith leaders can use to connect individuals with professional help.
- We are creating support groups within the faith community facilitated by mental health professionals, offering spiritual and psychological support.

The unity between faith and mental health services enhances individual support. It underscores the importance of seeking help as a display of strength and faith in healing possibilities.

As we wrap up this chapter, let's reflect on the impactful role of personal connections—peer support, family dynamics, educational settings, workplaces, or spiritual communities—in healing and perseverance. These support systems, built on empathy, understanding, and proactive steps, serve as the bedrock on which individuals can reconstruct their lives in the face of mental health obstacles. As we move ahead, let us embrace the lessons of empathy, harness the power of community, and maintain an unwavering faith in the potential for renewal and hope.

THE ESSENTIAL GUIDE TO SUICIDE PREVENTION

Transformative Strategies for Reducing Self-Harm, Enhancing Mental Health, and Building Personal Resilience

"The bravest thing I ever did was continuing my life when I wanted to die." — Juliette Lewis

"Sometimes even to live is an act of courage." — Seneca

"You are stronger than your challenges, and your challenges are making you stronger." — Karen Salmansohn

When we give without expecting anything in return, we lift others up, and in doing so, we find more joy in our own lives. Let's come together and make a difference.

Would you help someone just like you—someone who wants to learn more about **suicide prevention**, but isn't sure where to begin?

My mission is to make **understanding and practicing suicide prevention** something anyone can do. But to reach more people who need this, I need your help.

Most people choose books based on reviews. By leaving a review, you can help someone else find the hope and support they need. It's free, and it takes less than a minute, but it could change someone's life forever.

Your review could help...

...one more person find hope.
...one more family discover strength.
...one more life be saved.
...one more soul find the resilience to keep going.

To make a difference, simply scan the QR code below and leave a review:

If you love helping others, you're my kind of person. Thank you from the bottom of my heart!

Vernon Mullins, MSN, APRN, FNP-BC

FOUR

Navigating Through Grief and Healing

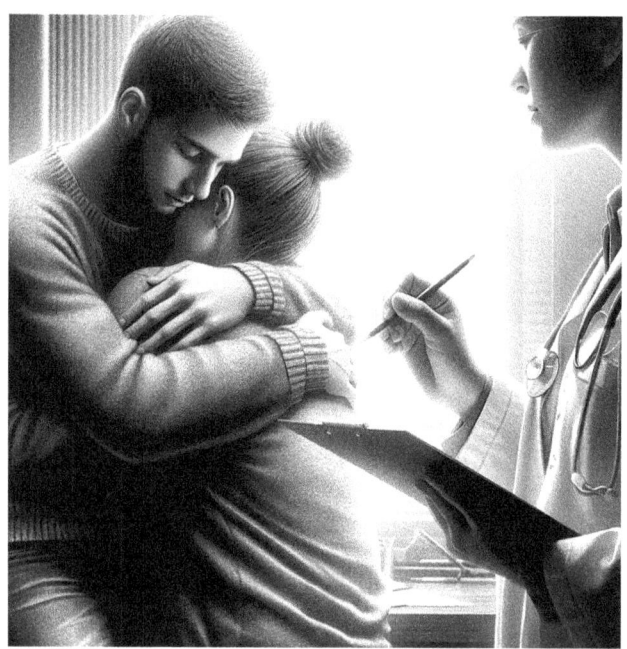

G rief is a storm that reshapes the landscape of our lives. It comes with its own seasons, which are unpredictable and unique to each person it touches. Amid this storm, we often search for a lighthouse—a guide to help us through the tumultuous waves. This chapter seeks to be that beacon, shedding light on the intricate grieving process, its broad spectrum of emotions, and how we can navigate these waters with grace and understanding.

4.1 Understanding the Grieving Process: A Guide for the Bereaved

Grief, in its essence, is love's unwillingness to let go. It's a profound response to loss, encompassing everything from the death of a loved one to the end of a significant life chapter. Here, we unfold the layers of the grieving process, acknowledging its complexity and the deeply personal journey it represents.

Stages of Grief

- **Denial**: A protective mechanism that helps us to survive the initial shock.
- **Anger**: A natural response to feeling powerless and unfairly deprived.
- **Bargaining**: A futile attempt to regain control by making deals with a higher power.
- **Depression**: A deep sense of sadness as the reality of the loss sets in.
- **Acceptance**: A gradual acknowledgment of the new reality, paving the way for moving forward.

It's important to remember that these stages are not linear. One may move between stages, experience several at once, or skip a stage entirely. The process is as unique as the individual experiencing it.

Normalizing a Range of Emotions

Grief can manifest as many emotions—anger, sadness, guilt, or even relief. Each emotion paints a stroke on the canvas of our grief, contributing to a picture that's entirely our own. Here are some common feelings:

- **Sadness**: An overwhelming sense of sorrow and longing.
- **Anger**: Frustration and irritation, sometimes directed at the person lost or those still here.
- **Guilt**: Regret over things said or unsaid, done or undone.
- **Relief**: Feeling relief, particularly after a prolonged illness, is not uncommon and doesn't diminish the love felt for the person lost.

Understanding that these emotions are natural can help you navigate them more gently.

The Individuality of Grief

If grief were a river, each person's journey down it would be in a different boat, at a different pace, and under different weather conditions. Some may find solace in solitude, while others seek comfort in community. Activities that provide a sense of normalcy or distraction might help one person but not another. The key is to find what feels right for you and allow yourself the grace to embrace it.

When to Seek Help

Recognizing when grief has become a storm too fierce to weather alone is vital. Here are some signs that professional support might be beneficial:

- **Prolonged Grieving**: When intense grief persists without signs of improvement, it may be time to seek help.
- **Functionality Impaired**: If grief significantly impacts your ability to perform daily tasks or maintain relationships, professional guidance can offer coping strategies.
- **Self-Harm Thoughts**: Thoughts of harming yourself are a clear signal that you need immediate support from a mental health professional.

Interactive Element: Grief Reflection Journal Prompts

Journaling can be a therapeutic tool for navigating grief. Here are some prompts to guide your reflections:

- **What emotion did I feel most strongly today?** Reflect on what triggered this emotion and how you responded to it.
- **What's one memory of my loved one that brought me comfort today?** Describe the memory and why it felt comforting.
- **What's one thing I wish I could say to my loved one right now?** Use this space to express those unsaid words.

Community Support Resource Elements:

- **Local Support Groups**: Many communities offer grief support groups, providing a space to share your experience with others who understand.
- **Counseling Services**: A list of reputable counseling services specializing in grief can guide you to professional support.

- **Online Forums**: Digital platforms where you can anonymously share your journey and receive support from a global community.

This chapter aims to be a compass through the storm of grief, acknowledging the pain, understanding the process, and gently guiding towards a healing path. Remember, grief is not a problem to be solved but a process to be lived through, with each person's journey as unique as the relationship they grieve.

4.2 Trauma-Informed Care: Principles and Practices

Acknowledging the silent echoes of past traumas is a pivotal step toward healing. Trauma-informed care (TIC) is a holistic approach that recognizes and responds to the effects of all types of trauma. It shifts the focus from asking, "What's wrong with you?" to "What happened to you?" This subtle yet profound change in perspective lays the foundation for building a supportive environment that fosters healing and empowerment.

Definition and Core Principles

Trauma-informed care is rooted in an understanding of the prevalence of trauma and its profound impact on an individual's life, health, and behavior. It encompasses five core principles designed to guide caregivers and service providers in creating a supportive framework for those they assist:

- **Safety**: Ensuring physical and emotional safety for individuals.
- **Trustworthiness and Transparency**: Building trust through consistent, transparent operations and interactions.

- **Peer Support**: Incorporating peer support and mutual self-help groups to establish safety and hope.
- **Collaboration and Mutuality**: Promoting equal participation and shared decision-making.
- **Empowerment, Voice, and Choice**: Recognizing individuals' strengths and experiences and empowering them with choices.

Implementing Trauma-Informed Practices

Incorporating TIC into various settings, from healthcare to community services, requires organizations to make a dedicated effort to adapt these principles into everyday practices. Here's how they can do it:

- **Training Staff**: Organizations must prioritize training for their staff to recognize the signs of trauma and respond appropriately.
- **Policy Revision**: Reviewing and revising policies and procedures to ensure they align with TIC principles, such as ensuring client safety and confidentiality.
- **Environment Check**: Adjusting the physical setting to make it feel safe, welcoming, and calming for individuals who may be sensitive to environmental triggers.
- **Feedback Systems**: Implementing systems for feedback and complaints that allow individuals to express concerns about their care, reinforcing their empowerment and voice.

The Role of Safety and Trust

Creating a foundation of safety and trust is essential for individuals who have experienced trauma. This begins with the physical environment, which should feel secure and welcoming but extends deeply into their interpersonal interactions with caregivers and service providers. Building trust requires consistency, patience, and an unwavering commitment to the individual's dignity and autonomy. This trust fosters a therapeutic alliance where individuals feel valued and understood, which is essential for navigating the path to healing.

- **Consistent Care**: Providing consistent care and support helps build a predictable environment where individuals can feel secure.
- **Active Listening**: Demonstrating active listening and genuine concern for the individual's story reinforces their worth and fosters trust.
- **Respecting Boundaries**: Recognizing and respecting personal boundaries is crucial for establishing a safe space for individuals to express themselves.

Empowerment in Healing

Empowerment is a cornerstone of TIC, where individuals are encouraged to participate actively in their healing journey. This involves recognizing their strengths and resilience, involving them in care planning, and supporting their right to choose treatment options. Here are some strategies to promote empowerment:

- **Strengths-Based Approach**: Focus on an individual's strengths rather than deficits to foster competence and resilience.
- **Informed Choices**: Ensure that caregivers fully inform individuals about their care options and support them in making choices that align with their values and preferences.

- **Skill Building**: Offer opportunities for individuals to build skills in communication, problem-solving, and self-care, enhancing their sense of agency and autonomy.

Trauma-informed care is not just a set of principles but a paradigm shift in the approach to healing and support. It acknowledges the pervasive impact of trauma and the strength of those who have experienced it. By fostering environments of safety, trust, and empowerment, we pave the way for individuals to reclaim their narratives and move forward with strength and resilience.

4.3 The Role of Therapy: Finding the Right Fit

In facing the aftermath of loss or trauma, engaging with therapy can be likened to finding a compass in uncharted territory. It's a tool, albeit a profoundly personal one, that can guide individuals through the complexities of their emotions and experiences. Not all therapies are created equal, nor do they fit every individual's needs in the same way. This exploration aims to illuminate the path to selecting the most resonant therapeutic approach and fostering a relationship with a therapist that nurtures healing.

Types of Therapy

Within the therapeutic field lies a diverse and abundant range of approaches, each characterized by its unique methods and areas of concentration. Below are some notable types:

- **Cognitive Behavioral Therapy (CBT)**: This method is grounded in the principle that our thoughts, feelings, and behaviors are interconnected. CBT works on identifying

and challenging unhelpful thought patterns to bring about positive changes in behavior and emotional state.
- **Dialectical Behavior Therapy (DBT)**: Originally developed for individuals with borderline personality disorder, DBT has proven effective for a broad range of issues. It emphasizes the development of coping skills, particularly in managing intense emotions and improving interpersonal relationships.
- **Narrative Therapy**: This approach centers on the stories we tell about our lives. Narrative therapy helps individuals reframe their experiences, highlighting their agency and the ability to rewrite their stories to acknowledge their strength and resilience.

Choosing the correct type of therapy is a critical first step on the healing path. It's essential to consider what resonates most with your current needs, whether altering detrimental thought patterns, enhancing emotional regulation, or reshaping your life narrative.

Finding a Therapist

Selecting a therapist who is a good match can feel daunting. Here are some practical tips to simplify this journey:

- **Research**: Start by investigating therapists' specialties and the types of therapy they offer. Many therapists provide information about their approach and focus areas on their websites or online directories.
- **Consultations**: Many therapists provide initial consultations, either free or at a reduced fee. Use this opportunity to ask about their experience with issues similar to yours, their approach to therapy, and any other questions that will help you gauge compatibility.

- **Listen to Your Gut**: Reflect on your feelings after a consultation or the first few sessions. Do you feel heard and understood? Do you believe this person can support you effectively? Your comfort and trust are paramount in this relationship.

The Therapeutic Relationship

The therapeutic alliance, the term often used to describe the relationship between a therapist and their client, is foundational to successful therapy. It thrives on the pillars of mutual respect, trust, and understanding. The strength of this alliance is a critical determinant in the healing journey, offering a sanctuary for openness and development. Essential elements of this alliance encompass:

- **Empathy**: Your therapist should demonstrate a deep understanding of your experiences and emotions.
- **Collaboration**: Therapy is a joint effort. You and your therapist should work together to set goals and navigate the healing process.
- **Respect for Boundaries**: A professional therapist maintains clear boundaries, ensuring the relationship supports your best interests.

This relationship, nurtured over time, becomes a vessel for profound change and healing.

Online Therapy Options

With the advent of technology, online therapy has emerged as a flexible and accessible option for many. It breaks down barriers related to location, mobility, and scheduling, making it an attractive choice for those who might not engage in traditional face-to-face therapy. Considerations for online treatment include:

- **Convenience and Accessibility**: Online therapy can be conducted from anywhere, offering solutions for those with busy schedules or limited access to local mental health services.
- **Selection of Therapists**: The digital platform allows you to widen the pool of available therapists, helping you find someone who truly fits your needs, even if they're not located in your immediate area.
- **Privacy and Comfort**: Engaging in therapy from the comfort of your home can reduce anxiety for some, making it easier to open up about sensitive topics.

However, it's essential to weigh these benefits against potential limitations:

- **Connection Issues**: Technical difficulties can disrupt sessions, potentially impacting the flow of conversation and emotional connection.
- **Privacy Concerns**: Ensuring a private, uninterrupted space for sessions at home can be challenging for some.
- **Differences in Communication**: Non-verbal cues can be more complex to read in a virtual setting, which might affect some individuals' depth of the therapeutic relationship.

In conclusion, the journey through grief and trauma is deeply personal, and the role of therapy within that journey is pivotal. Whether choosing between CBT, DBT, narrative therapy, or another approach, the essence lies in finding a path that resonates with your individual needs. Equally, selecting a therapist —

someone who will walk beside you on this path — requires careful consideration of their approach, your comfort with them, and the strength of the therapeutic relationship. Online options further expand these possibilities, offering flexibility and accessibility to those seeking support. In navigating these choices, you lay the groundwork for a healing journey that is as unique and individual as your own story.

4.4 Navigating the Complexities of Survivor's Guilt

Survivor's guilt manifests in those who have lived through tragedies that others have not. It's a complex emotional storm, filled with questions like "Why me?" and "What if?". This burden does not solely afflict survivors of accidents or wars; it also weighs heavily on anyone who feels they have unjustly survived where others have perished. In this discussion, we delve into the intricacies of survivor's guilt, guiding readers toward a journey of self-forgiveness and acceptance through its challenging terrain.

Survivor's guilt arises when individuals believe they have done something wrong by surviving a traumatic event that others did not. This guilt can manifest from surviving accidents, natural disasters, conflicts, or the loss of loved ones to illnesses. It gnaws on the psyche, questioning one's right to happiness, well-being, or even life itself. The 'why' behind its occurrence is complex, intertwining feelings of responsibility, randomness of survival, and deep-seated notions of fairness and justice.

Strategies for Coping

To navigate the rocky terrain of survivor's guilt, several strategies can serve as guideposts:

- **Acknowledgement and Acceptance**: The first step is to recognize the presence of survivor's guilt. Accept that these feelings, however unwarranted they seem, are a natural response to what you've endured.
- **Expression**: Find a medium to express your feelings. Whether through talking to a trusted person, writing in a journal, or creating art, expression can be a release valve for the pent-up emotions of guilt.
- **Reframing Thoughts**: Challenge the guilt-inducing thoughts with reality checks. For instance, remind yourself that survival wasn't a choice made at the expense of others but a random twist of fate.
- **Connecting with Others**: Engage with people who've gone through similar experiences. Their journey through survivor's guilt can offer insights, comfort, and a sense of not being alone in your feelings.
- **Contributing Positively**: Channel the energy from your guilt into positive action. Volunteering, advocating for causes related to the tragedy, or helping others affected can be therapeutic.

The Role of Self-Compassion

Self-compassion involves treating yourself with the same kindness and understanding you would offer a friend in distress. Here's how to cultivate self-compassion:

- **Mindfulness**: Be aware of your thoughts and feelings without judgment. Recognize that survivor's guilt is a part of your experience but doesn't define your worth.
- **Self-kindness**: Be gentle with yourself. Acknowledge your suffering and offer yourself words of encouragement and comfort.

- **Common Humanity**: Understand that you're not alone. Many have walked this path before you, and their resilience can be a source of inspiration.

Seeking Support

While the journey through survivor's guilt is deeply personal, it's a path not meant to be walked alone. Seeking support can illuminate the way forward:

- **Therapy**: A therapist, especially one specializing in trauma, can help unravel the complex emotions tied to a survivor's guilt. Therapeutic approaches such as Cognitive Behavioral Therapy (CBT) and Eye Movement Desensitization and Reprocessing (EMDR) have shown efficacy in addressing trauma-related guilt.
- **Peer Support Groups**: Groups dedicated to survivors provide a community of understanding and empathy. Sharing your story and hearing others can lessen the isolation that often accompanies survivor's guilt.
- **Spiritual or Religious Guidance**: For some, spiritual or religious support offers a framework to understand and cope with their guilt. Engaging with a community that shares your spiritual beliefs can provide comfort and peace.

In navigating the complexities of survivor's guilt, remember that healing is not a destination but a process. It involves winding paths, setbacks, and discoveries. Each step, whether forward or backward, is a part of moving through the guilt toward a place where you can honor those lost by living fully. The path to healing doesn't involve eliminating guilt but embracing it as a part of your story. It's about transforming this guilt into a catalyst for personal development, fostering a more profound sense of empathy, and building resilience.

4.5 Healing Rituals and Remembrance: Honoring Loved Ones

In the aftermath of loss, our hearts and minds search for ways to hold onto the essence of those who have left us. This quest for connection often leads us to create rituals and acts of remembrance. Deeply personal or shared practices serve as bridges between our past with our loved ones and our present without them. They offer comfort, a sense of continuity, and a means to honor the depth of our relationships.

Creating Personal Rituals

Personal rituals can be as unique as the relationship they commemorate. These practices don't have to be elaborate but should hold personal meaning and bring to mind cherished memories. Below are some suggestions to help you create your meaningful rituals:

- **Lighting a Candle**: Choose a specific time each day or on meaningful dates to light a candle in memory of your loved one. Lighting it and watching the flame flicker can serve as a moment of reflection and connection.
- **Writing Letters**: Penning letters to your loved one can provide a cathartic outlet for expressing feelings, sharing updates, or simply saying the things left unsaid. These letters can be kept, buried, or ceremonially burned.
- **Planting a Garden**: Select flowers, shrubs, or trees that remind you of the person you've lost. Tending to this garden becomes an ongoing ritual that honors their memory through growth and beauty.

Cultural and Religious Rituals

Across cultures and faiths, rituals surrounding death and remembrance reflect the diversity of human expression. Exploring these practices can broaden our understanding and inspire our own acts of remembrance.

- **Dia de los Muertos**: This Mexican tradition blends Indigenous and Catholic practices. It involves creating altars with offerings to welcome the spirits of the deceased back for a yearly visit.
- **Memorial Stones**: In Jewish tradition, placing stones on graves serves as a sign of respect and remembrance, symbolizing the lasting presence of loved ones in our lives.
- **Bon Festival**: In Japan, this Buddhist observance invites families to clean their ancestors' graves and prepare special meals in honor of their spirits, believed to visit the living during this time.

By exploring these diverse traditions, we uncover the universal threads of love, remembrance, and the eternal cycle of life and death that bind us all. Infusing personal rituals with elements that speak to you deepens their meaning and strengthens your connection to the memory of your loved ones.

The Role of Memorials

Memorials, whether physical structures, digital spaces, or simple acts of creation, serve as focal points for both collective and individual grieving. They provide a tangible connection to those we've lost and offer a place or way to direct our grief and memories.

- **Physical Memorials**: Plaques, benches, or sculptures in public spaces allow for a communal sharing of grief and offer a place for reflection and homage.
- **Digital Memorials**: Digital platforms that enable the sharing of memories, photographs, and messages, creating a vivid and heartfelt portrait of a loved one's life that surpasses geographical boundaries.
- **Creative Acts**: Composing music, painting, or writing poetry in honor of a loved one transforms grief into artistic expression, capturing emotions in a form that endures.

The creation and maintenance of these memorials are rituals in themselves, evolving over time as we process our loss and integrate the memory of our loved ones into our lives.

Anniversaries and Milestones

Navigating significant dates such as birthdays, anniversaries, or holidays can be particularly challenging in the wake of loss, as they often can revive our sense of grief. These events, while challenging, also offer unique opportunities for healing. It's important to strike a delicate balance—recognizing and respecting our emotions while also finding meaningful ways to honor the memories of our loved ones.

- **Plan Ahead**: Anticipate the emotional impact of these dates. Decide how you wish to spend the day, whether in solitude, with family, or participating in an activity that holds special meaning.
- **Create a Tradition**: Establish new traditions incorporating your loved one's memory. These traditions could be as simple as preparing their favorite meal, visiting

a place they enjoyed together, or performing an act of kindness in their name.
- **Allow for Flexibility**: Your needs may change from year to year. Honor where you are each time an anniversary comes around, allowing yourself the freedom to adapt your plans.

Integrating these practices into our lives weaves a rich tapestry of memories, love, and the enduring spirit of those we've lost. Rituals and remembrances not only honor our relationships but also embed the essence of our loved ones into our daily existence. This legacy symbolizes the depth of our bonds and the resilience of the human spirit amidst loss.

4.6 Journaling as a Tool for Healing

Journaling emerges as a powerful ally in the healing process in quiet moments of reflection. This simple yet profound practice offers a private sanctuary for thoughts, emotions, and memories, providing a tangible form to the intangible journey of grief and trauma recovery. Through the written word, journaling enables individuals to explore their inner landscape, finding clarity and solace amidst the chaos of loss.

Benefits of Journaling

Journaling offers benefits that reach beyond simply putting words on paper. This practice acts as a mirror, reflecting the complexity of our emotions and experiences and fostering a deeper understanding and acceptance of our feelings.

- **Emotional Release**: Writing provides an outlet for bottled-up emotions, relieving the pressure of unexpressed feelings.
- **Clarity and Insight**: Writing down thoughts can help untangle them, offering new perspectives and insights into our grief and feelings that may not have been fully understood or explored.
- **Memory Preservation**: Journaling can serve to capture memories of loved ones, preserving the details and moments we fear might fade with time.
- **Stress Reduction**: Research shows that writing lowers stress levels and improves mental and physical well-being.

Starting a Grief Journal

Crafting a journal tailored to this chapter of your life can be a powerful resource to guide you through the distinctive journey of grief and loss. Starting a dedicated grief journal may seem overwhelming initially, but by following a few straightforward steps, you can establish a secure and supportive space for your healing process.

- **Choose Your Medium**: Whether a traditional notebook, a digital document, or a specialized journaling app, select a medium that feels comfortable, emotionally, and accessible.
- **Create a Routine**: Setting aside a regular time for journaling can help integrate this practice into your daily life. Even just a few minutes each day can make a significant difference.
- **No Rules**: Remember, journaling has no rules. Your entries can be as long or as short as needed, written in any style that feels right.

Expressive Writing

Just like journaling, expressive writing goes beyond merely jotting down events or emotions; it delves into a profound, personal investigation of one's thoughts and feelings. This writing style can offer a distinctive blend of creativity and personality as a means of emotional expression, providing an unconventional avenue for individuals to navigate and comprehend their experiences.

- **Focus on Feelings**: Let yourself delve into what happened and how it made you feel. Articulating emotions can lead to a deeper understanding and eventual acceptance.
- **Explore the Unexplored**: Don't shy away from the hard or uncomfortable feelings. Writing about them can help to diminish their power over you.
- **Look for Growth**: Reflect on personal growth or insights gained through your experiences. Recognizing these can foster a sense of progress and resilience.

Privacy and Sharing

The privacy of a journal offers a space free from judgment, where one can express one's innermost thoughts and feelings without fear. This sanctuary is crucial for those navigating the rawness of grief and trauma.

- **Guard Your Privacy**: If you're concerned about others reading your journal, take steps to ensure its privacy. These steps include keeping it in a locked location or using password-protected digital documents.
- **Choose to Share (or Not)**: While the journal is primarily for you, sharing some of your entries with a trusted friend, family member, or therapist can be therapeutic. It provides

an opportunity for connection and can help others understand your journey.
- **Reflect on the Process**: Periodically, look back on your past entries. This reflection can offer valuable insights into your healing journey, showing how your feelings and perspectives have evolved over time.

Journaling serves as a powerful testament to human resilience, beautifully honoring the complexity of our pain and experiences. It fosters a silent yet profound dialogue between the individual and the written word, acting as a steadfast companion through the healing journey. This practice witnesses our evolution amidst grief and provides a unique lifeline, deeply connecting us to our innermost selves. It offers comfort, insight, and a path forward, transcending traditional writing boundaries.

4.7 The Impact of Community Memorials and Vigils

In times of loss, the community comes together to offer support, sharing in each other's sadness and understanding. Community memorials and gatherings are vital in this support system, serving as essential places for people to mourn and remember together. These events honor the memory of those we've lost and help everyone heal together, blending individual grief into a sense of shared resilience.

Collective Grieving

The act of mourning, while deeply personal, finds a universal expression through community memorials and vigils. These events allow us to step outside the isolation of our grief, offering our sorrows to the shared embrace of our community. Here, in these gatherings, the silent weight of loss finds a voice articulated through the collective mourning of those gathered. The power of this shared experience lies in remembering and the communal acknowledgment of loss, reaffirming that no one grieves alone.

- Shared stories and memories of the departed weave a communal narrative, reminding us of the impact one life can have on many.
- The collective expression of grief, through tears, music, or silence, helps normalize the vast array of emotions that loss invokes, providing a safe space for all forms of mourning.

Creating a Sense of Unity

Community memorials and vigils act as a gathering point, bringing together people from diverse backgrounds with a shared goal of honoring and remembering. This deep connection bridges differences to find commonality in the universal feeling of loss. The unity created in these instances showcases the resilience of community ties, formed through shared grief and lasting long after.

- From holding hands to collective singing, solidarity reinforces a sense of belonging and support among those present.
- The shared experience of loss becomes a foundation for new connections, as individuals find comfort and understanding in the presence of others who have experienced similar pain.

Planning Meaningful Memorials

Crafting a memorial or vigil that genuinely respects the memory of those who have passed while offering comfort to the bereaved requires a careful blend of empathy and inventiveness. Consider the following guidelines to make these ceremonies resonate deeply and respectfully with everyone involved:

- **Inclusivity**: Ensure the planning process is open, allowing input from various community members to reflect the community's diversity and the multifaceted impact of the loss.
- **Personalization**: Incorporate elements that speak to the unique lives of those being remembered—be it through music, readings, or visual displays—making the memorial a true reflection of their essence.
- **Accessibility**: Consider the needs of all community members and ensure the location and timing of the event are accessible to those who wish to participate.
- **Continuity**: Consider ways the memorial or vigil can have a lasting impact, such as establishing a scholarship, planting a memorial garden, or creating a permanent physical monument. This ongoing legacy offers a tangible reminder of the lives commemorated and the unity forged in their memory.

At the core of every community is an inherent ability to offer profound compassion and engage in collective healing processes. By organizing and participating in memorials and vigils, we do more than remember those who have departed; we strengthen the bonds that unite us. Such events are significant markers in our shared journey, highlighting our experiences of grief while emphasizing our dedication to mutual support, remembrance, and collective recovery.

4.8 The Healing Power of Nature: Ecotherapy Insights

In our fast-paced world, we often need to catch up with nature's calming presence, overlooking its potential for healing and rejuvenation. Ecotherapy, a term that has blossomed in the realm of psychological healing, offers another unique pathway to healing. This section explores how nature immersion can heal the soul's wounds, providing comfort and fortitude during difficult times.

Nature as a Healing Space

Ecotherapy rests on the foundational belief that engagement with the earth's landscapes is not merely a leisure activity but a vital component of emotional and mental health. The concept isn't novel; many cultures have long recognized the significance of the natural world in maintaining balance and harmony within the human spirit. It is an acknowledgment of how nature's rhythm–its growth, decay, and rebirth cycles – mirrors our healing and recovery processes. The tranquility of a forest, the river's resilience, and the ocean's vastness can serve as powerful metaphors for our journey through grief and loss, reminding us of the continuity of life and the potential for renewal within ourselves.

Activities for Connection

Connecting with nature as a form of therapy presents diverse options, mirroring the vastness and variety of the natural world itself. The following activities exemplify ways to foster this meaningful relationship:

- **Hiking**: Hiking can facilitate eco-healing in the grieving process by offering a peaceful environment in which to find solace and connect with nature. Engaging with the natural world during hikes allows for reflection, emotional release, and a renewed sense of connection, aiding in the healing journey through grief.
- **Gardening**: Nurturing plants, from sowing seeds to witnessing their growth, can be a profound exercise in hope and a metaphor for personal growth.
- **Beachcombing**: The rhythmic sound of waves and searching for treasures along the shoreline can be soothing, offering a sense of serenity and mindfulness.

The Science Behind Nature's Impact

The positive impact of nature on mental health extends beyond personal stories into the realm of scientific evidence. Research consistently demonstrates that time spent in natural settings can significantly decrease stress, anxiety, and depression levels. Natural environments have been scientifically associated with lower blood pressure, reduced heart rates, and a decrease in the production of stress hormones, underscoring the physical underpinnings of nature's soothing effects. Furthermore, natural immersion improves cognitive performance, enhances concentration and attention, and elevates mood. The Attention Restoration Theory posits that natural environments rejuvenate the mind, revitalizing cognitive abilities worn down by contemporary life's relentless pace.

Incorporating Nature into Daily Life

Finding ways to connect with nature is challenging for those residing in urban environments, where concrete often overshadows greenery. However, even in the city's heart, opportunities to weave elements of the natural world into our daily lives abound. Here are some suggestions:

- **Indoor Plants**: Bringing plants into your home or workspace can introduce a touch of nature's vitality. The care involved in maintaining them also fosters a nurturing connection.
- **Urban Green Spaces**: Seek out parks, community gardens, or waterfronts within your city. Regular visits offer a respite from the urban grind and a dose of nature's tranquility.
- **Nature Sounds**: Use apps or recordings of nature sounds —such as rain, ocean waves, or forest ambiance—to create a calming environment in your living or workspace.
- **Micro-Adventures**: Plan short excursions to nearby natural attractions. A day trip to a state park, botanical garden, or nature reserve can provide a meaningful connection with the natural world.

In an age where disconnection and distraction prevail, ecotherapy can help provide a timeless healing path that remains relevant and effective in today's fast-paced world.

4.9 Art Therapy: Expressing the Inexpressible

In the healing process, especially for feelings that are hard to put into words, art therapy serves as a pathway to express the unspeakable, turning emotional turmoil into tangible creations. This therapy encourages individuals to explore and convey their inner feelings through art, offering a unique way to understand and heal beyond conventional words.

Art as a Means of Expression

Art therapy operates on the principle that creative expression can unearth and communicate feelings that might otherwise remain buried. It provides an alternative language for those navigating the aftermath of loss or trauma. This mode of expression can be particularly liberating for individuals who find verbal communication of their experiences challenging or insufficient. Through creation, emotions find their shape, colors, and textures, allowing for a tangible encounter with one's inner reality.

Different Forms of Art Therapy

The beauty of art therapy lies in its diversity. It offers a spectrum of mediums to suit individual preferences and resonances, each providing a unique avenue for exploration and expression.

- **Drawing**: With simple tools like pencils and paper, drawing offers an immediate and accessible way to externalize thoughts and feelings.
- **Painting**: Paint's fluidity allows for the deep exploration of emotions, with colors and strokes mirroring the complexity of personal experiences.
- **Sculpture**: Working with materials like clay or found objects, sculpture engages the sense of touch, grounding individuals in the present while they shape their narratives.
- **Digital Art**: For those more inclined towards technology, digital art platforms offer endless possibilities for creativity without physical art supplies.

These varied forms of art therapy ensure that there's a medium for everyone, regardless of their artistic inclination or experience. The key lies in finding the form that resonates most deeply, providing a comfortable and expressive outlet for the journey through healing.

No Artistic Skills Required

Many people mistakenly believe that art therapy requires artistic prowess or talent, but this is far from the truth. Art therapy emphasizes the journey of creation over the final result. The actual healing aspect comes from self-expression, not from the artistic proficiency of the outcome.

- Participants are encouraged to let go of judgments about their artistic ability and embrace the act of creation as a means of exploration and expression.
- The emphasis is on the emotional and psychological significance of the artwork, valuing personal meaning over technical skill.

4.10 Moving Forward: Rebuilding Life After Loss

Navigating through loss can feel like piecing together a puzzle scattered apart, daunting at first glance. However, in this process lies the potential for growth, transformation, and a redefinition of what we perceive as our new normal. Moving forward isn't about going back to who we were before the loss but about evolving into the person we are becoming in its wake.

Redefining Normal

The concept of a "new normal" captures the essence of life after loss. It acknowledges that the landscape of our lives has changed irrevocably, and that moving forward requires us to navigate this altered terrain. This new normal is not a destination but a process of adaptation, where we learn to integrate our experiences of loss into the ongoing narrative of our lives. It's about finding ways to continue living fully, even in the shadow of our grief.

- Acceptance plays a vital role in this process. It allows us to acknowledge our loss without letting it define us.
- Flexibility is crucial as we discover that our needs and responses may change over time.
- We need patience with ourselves and understanding that this redefinition is a gradual process, not a quick fix.

Setting New Goals and Intentions

Adjusting to our circumstances involves establishing fresh objectives and aspirations to steer us forward. These aims don't have to be grandiose; they could be as straightforward as finding happiness in everyday moments or as meaningful as revisiting a long-held aspiration. Setting these targets signifies our resolve to endure our loss and flourish in its wake.

- Short-term goals can offer immediate focus points, providing a sense of accomplishment and forward momentum.
- Long-term intentions can guide our broader healing journey, helping us envision a future with meaning and possibility.

Support Networks in Moving Forward

The journey through grief and rebuilding is not one we need to make alone. Leaning on old and new support networks can provide the compassion, understanding, and encouragement necessary to navigate this path. These networks, be they our family, friends, support groups, or mental health professionals, offer a range of supportive measures to sustain us when finding our balance is challenging.

- Existing relationships can offer a foundation of familiarity and comfort, grounding us in a sense of continuity.
- New connections, forged through shared experiences of loss or healing, can provide fresh perspectives and mutual support.

As we journey forward from loss, we intricately piece our cherished memories, current experiences, and future aspirations into a collage that celebrates our growth and honors those we've mourned. This process, essential for our sense of self, involves reshaping our understanding of normalcy, charting new paths that align with our dreams, maintaining connections with those who have passed, and drawing on the surrounding support. As we close this chapter, we reflect on reconstructing life post-loss as a deeply personal and communal journey. It showcases our resilience, quest for optimism amidst sorrow, and enduring love that transcends grief. Each step we take incorporates our encounters with loss into the essence of who we are, enriching our story with depth, vibrancy, and fortitude.

FIVE

Empowering Change: Suicide Prevention in Action

The moment a firefighter rushes into a blaze or a lifeguard dives into turbulent waters; there's no question they're there to save lives. It's less often we picture these same heroes poised on the edge of a conversation, ready to pull someone back from the brink of a mental health crisis. Yet, the reality is that first responders are on the front lines of suicide prevention, often as the first point of contact for individuals in acute distress. Their role is as critical as it is complex, requiring bravery, compassion, understanding, and specialized training to navigate these delicate situations effectively.

5.1 Suicide Prevention Training: Empowering First Responders

Critical Role of First Responders

Imagine the police officer who finds someone standing on a bridge, not there to enjoy the view but contemplating jumping. Or paramedics who respond to a call from someone who thought they wanted to end it all, but now they're scared because the pills they took are starting to work. These professionals need to do more than show up; they need to connect, communicate, and care in a way that makes a real difference at that critical moment.

Training Content and Techniques

For first responders, practical suicide prevention training covers a lot more ground than most people realize. It's about more than what to say but how to listen. Courses often include:

- **Risk Assessment**: Understanding how to quickly and accurately assess the risk of suicide.
- **Communication Skills**: Learning the art of speaking to someone in crisis means often talking less and listening more.

- **De-escalation Techniques**: Calming the situation, reducing the immediate risk, and making it safe to talk about options.
- **Referral and Follow-Up**: Knowing what resources are available and how to connect individuals with the help they need.

Scenario-Based Learning

It's one thing to learn about these techniques in a classroom; it's another to apply them in real life. That's where scenario-based training comes in. It places first responders in simulated situations that mirror what they might face, from crisis calls to family interventions. This hands-on practice builds confidence and competence, ensuring they're ready when every second counts.

- **Real-World Scenarios**: Training includes simulations based on real-life situations, providing practical experience in handling diverse crises.
- **Feedback and Reflection**: After each scenario, trainers provide feedback, allowing for reflection on what worked, what didn't, and why.

Impact on Suicide Prevention Rates

Research shows that when first responders receive targeted training in suicide prevention, the outcomes can be significant. A study published in the *Journal of Crisis Intervention and Suicide Prevention* highlighted a marked decrease in suicide rates in communities where first responders were trained in these specialized techniques. The presence of a knowledgeable and compassionate first responder can be the turning point, moving an individual from despair to hope.

- **Lower Suicide Rates**: Communities with trained first responders see a decrease in suicide rates.
- **Increased Help-Seeking**: People are more likely to seek help if they encounter a first responder who understands their crisis and can offer support.

Training as a Lifeline

The call to serve as a first responder is a call to be on the front lines of many crises, including those of mental health. With the proper training, these professionals save lives physically and safeguard the mental and emotional well-being of those they serve. It's a reminder that sometimes, our most powerful life-saving tool is the ability to connect, understand, and offer hope. Through comprehensive suicide prevention training, first responders are equipped with this tool, ready to make a difference when it matters most.

5.2 The Role of Media in Shaping Suicide Awareness

With its pervasive reach and influence, the media holds a unique position in our society. It reflects our world back to us and shapes our perceptions, beliefs, and understanding. This power, when harnessed with care and responsibility, can play an instrumental role in suicide prevention. It's about balancing informing the public and avoiding disseminating content that could potentially cause harm.

Responsible Reporting

When it comes to reporting on suicide, the stakes are exceptionally high. Words matter, and the way we tell stories can have profound implications. Guidelines for responsible reporting emphasize:

- Avoid sensationalism: Steering clear of dramatic headlines or imagery that glamorizes or oversimplifies suicide.
- Using appropriate language: Choosing words that do not stigmatize those who have died by suicide or their families.
- Excluding details: Omitting specific methods or locations to prevent copycat incidents, a phenomenon known as suicide contagion.
- Providing resources: Including information about where people can find help, reminding readers that support is available.

These principles do not concern censorship but ensure that the media contributes ethically and effectively to suicide prevention efforts.

Media as an Educational Tool

Beyond responsible reporting, the media has the capacity to educate and enlighten. Through documentaries, news features, and public service announcements, it can:

- Illuminate the complexities of mental health issues, debunking myths and reducing stigma.
- Share stories of hope and recovery, showing that suicide is not an inevitable outcome of crisis or mental illness.
- Highlight the importance of seeking help, emphasizing that mental health is just as important as physical health.

This educational role is crucial. It increases public awareness and fosters a more compassionate and informed society.

Collaboration with Mental Health Professionals

For the media to fulfill its potential as a force for good in suicide prevention, collaboration with mental health professionals is critical. This partnership can ensure that content is:

- Accurate: Ensure that the information about suicide and mental health is based on the latest research and best practices.
- Sensitive: Approaching stories with the understanding and empathy the subject requires.
- Helpful: Providing viewers or readers with actionable advice and resources.

Joint efforts, such as advisory panels or consultations, can help media professionals navigate the complexities of reporting on suicide, ensuring that their work contributes positively to public discourse.

Success Stories

There are numerous instances where media campaigns have made a tangible difference in the fight against suicide. For example:

- A national campaign that combined compelling storytelling with clear messaging on seeking help saw a significant uptick in calls to suicide prevention hotlines.
- A documentary series that followed the recovery journeys of several individuals living with mental illness resulted in increased public engagement with mental health services.
- An online platform that shares personal stories of resilience and recovery has become a go-to resource for those seeking inspiration and support.

These success stories underscore the media's potential to be a powerful ally in suicide prevention. The media can help break down barriers, open conversations, and save lives through responsible reporting, educational content, and collaboration with experts.

Interactive Element: Reflection Questions for Content Creators

- How can your work contribute to a more informed and compassionate conversation about suicide?
- What steps can you take to ensure that your reporting or storytelling is both sensitive and responsible?
- How might you leverage your platform to provide resources and support to those affected by suicide?

Textual Element: Checklist for Responsible Reporting on Suicide

- Avoid sensational language or imagery.
- Omit specific details about the method or location.
- Use appropriate, non-stigmatizing language.
- Include information on where to find help.

These elements, woven throughout media practices, can transform the landscape of suicide prevention, turning potential harm into hope and despair into dialogue.

5.3 Implementing School-Based Suicide Prevention Programs

Schools are more than just places of learning; they are crucial communities where young individuals spend a significant portion of their day, making them pivotal settings for identifying and addressing mental health issues, including suicidal ideation among students. The implementation of comprehensive suicide prevention programs within these educational environments can play a crucial role in safeguarding the well-being of students.

Early Intervention

Detecting signs of suicidal ideation at an early stage within the school environment is critical. Teachers and school staff, who interact with students daily, are ideally positioned to notice subtle behavior, mood, or academic performance changes that may indicate a student is at risk. Training programs designed to equip school personnel to identify these warning signs and understand the appropriate steps can be life-saving. Key aspects include:

- Developing clear protocols for when and how to report concerns about a student.
- Encouraging an atmosphere where students feel safe disclosing their feelings.
- Regular screening is part of the health services provided by the school.

Program Components

Effective school-based suicide prevention programs encompass several key components, each aimed at creating a supportive environment where students are educated about mental health and feel empowered to seek help. These components include:

- **Education**: Integrating mental health education into the curriculum to foster an understanding among students that mental health is an integral part of their overall well-being.

- **Training**: Providing specialized training for staff and educators on how to respond to mental health crises, including the development of intervention skills.
- **Peer Support Initiatives**: Establishing peer support networks within the school to offer students a platform where they can share experiences and support each other under the supervision of trained adults.
- **Crisis Management**: Developing and implementing a crisis management plan that includes procedures for immediate response, communication strategies, and postvention support to address the school community's needs in the aftermath of a suicide or attempted suicide.

Engaging Stakeholders

The success of suicide prevention programs is significantly enhanced when schools actively engage a wide range of stakeholders in their efforts. This collaborative approach ensures a comprehensive student support system that extends beyond the classroom. Strategies for stakeholder engagement include:

- **Involving Parents and Families**: Keeping parents informed about the school's suicide prevention initiatives and providing them with resources to support mental health at home.
- **Empowering Students**: Encouraging student participation in developing and implementing suicide prevention activities to ensure they resonate with the student body.
- **Partnering with Community Organizations**: Forming partnerships with local mental health organizations, clinics, and service providers to support the school's prevention efforts and facilitate referrals when necessary.

Interactive Workshop Plan for Teachers and Parents

Next is a sample that can be used as a template for structuring how an organization can model an interactive workshop aimed at teachers and parents, focusing on mental health awareness, identifying warning signs of suicidal ideation, and effective communication strategies with students and children. Feel free to adjust and adapt this sample workshop plan to fit your organization's needs.

SAMPLE TEMPLATE:

Interactive Workshop: "Understanding Mental Health, Identifying Warning Signs, and Effective Communication"

Welcome to our interactive workshop designed to empower teachers and parents with the knowledge and skills necessary to support mental health and prevent suicide among students and children.

Workshop Overview:

Objective: To enhance understanding of mental health, recognize warning signs of suicidal ideation, and develop effective communication strategies.

Agenda:

1. **Introduction to Mental Health** (*10 minutes*)

- Define mental health and its significance in academic and personal growth.

- Discuss common mental health challenges faced by children and adolescents.

2. **Recognizing Warning Signs of Suicidal Ideation** (*15 minutes*)

    - Educate participants on key indicators of potential suicidal behavior.
    - Provide examples and case studies to illustrate warning signs effectively.

3. **Effective Communication Strategies** (*20 minutes*)

    - Explore strategies for fostering open and supportive dialogues with students and children.
    - Role-playing exercises to practice active listening and communication techniques.

4. **Q&A Session and Discussion** (*10 minutes*)

    - Address participant questions and concerns related to mental health and suicide prevention.
    - Encourage open dialogue and sharing of personal experiences or challenges.

5. **Resources and Support Services** (*5 minutes*)

    - Share information on local mental health resources, crisis hotlines, and support services.
    - Provide handouts and educational materials for further reference.

Key Takeaways:

- Increased awareness of mental health issues and their significance.
- Improved ability to recognize warning signs of suicidal ideation.
- Enhanced communication skills for engaging with students or children on sensitive topics.

Conclusion:

Thank you for your dedication to promoting mental health and preventing suicide. By participating in this workshop, you have taken a vital step towards creating a safer and more supportive environment for our youth.

Measuring Impact

To ensure the continued effectiveness and relevance of school-based suicide prevention programs, educators and administrators must employ methods that accurately assess their impact. This assessment can guide necessary adjustments and improvements to the programs. Approaches to measuring impact include:

- **Pre and Post Surveys**: Conduct anonymous surveys among students and staff before and after the implementation of the program to gauge changes in awareness, attitudes, and self-reported behavior regarding mental health and suicide prevention.

- **Incident Tracking**: Keeping records of reported incidents of suicidal ideation, attempts, and related mental health crises to monitor trends over time.
- **Feedback Loops**: Creating channels for regular feedback from students, parents, and educators about the program's effectiveness and areas for enhancement.

Resource List for School-Based Suicide Prevention

Here is a comprehensive list of resources, websites, toolkits, and guides specifically tailored to support schools in developing, implementing, and evaluating suicide prevention programs, as well as training materials and educational content suitable for staff and students:

1. **The Suicide Prevention Resource Center (SPRC)** - Offers a wealth of resources, toolkits, and guides for developing and implementing suicide prevention programs in schools. Visit: [SPRC] (https://www.sprc.org/)
2. **American Foundation for Suicide Prevention (AFSP)** - Provides educational materials, training programs, and school resources to address suicide prevention. Visit: [AFSP School Resources] (https://afsp.org/suicide-prevention-resources/)
3. **JED Foundation** - Focuses on promoting emotional health and preventing suicide among teens and young adults. Their resources include guidance for schools on creating comprehensive mental health and suicide prevention programs. Visit: [JED Foundation] (https://www.jedfoundation.org/)
4. **National Alliance on Mental Illness (NAMI)** - Offers education and training programs, including resources for schools to address mental health and suicide prevention.

Visit: [NAMI's Education Programs] (https://www.nami.org/Support-Education)
5. **National Institute of Mental Health (NIMH)** - Provides evidence-based information on mental health, including resources for schools looking to implement suicide prevention initiatives. Visit: [NIMH School Resources] (https://www.nimh.nih.gov/health/topics/suicide-prevention/index.shtml)
6. **The Trevor Project** - Focuses on suicide prevention among LGBTQ+ youth and offers educational resources and training for schools. Visit: [The Trevor Project] (https://www.thetrevorproject.org/)
7. **SAMHSA's Preventing Suicide: A Toolkit for High Schools** - A comprehensive toolkit for high schools to develop and implement suicide prevention strategies. Access the toolkit: (https://store.samhsa.gov/product/Preventing-Suicide-A-Toolkit-for-High-Schools/SMA12-4669)
8. **Crisis Text Line** - Provides free, 24/7 crisis support via text message. Students and staff can access immediate help by texting "HELLO" to 741741. Visit: (https://www.crisistextline.org/)
9. **American School Counselor Association (ASCA)** - Offers resources, webinars, and best practices for school counselors focusing on mental health and suicide prevention. Visit: [ASCA] (https://www.schoolcounselor.org/)
10. **The Jason Foundation** - Provides educational programs and resources specifically aimed at preventing youth suicide. Visit: [The Jason Foundation Resources] (https://www.jasonfoundation.com/)

These resources offer a range of tools, guides, and educational materials to support schools in developing, implementing, and evaluating effective suicide prevention programs. Explore each of these sources to find the most relevant materials for your school community.

5.4 Holistic Approaches to Mental Health: Beyond Traditional Therapy

We've learned that one size does not fit all in healing and well-being. The beauty of holistic approaches to mental health lies in their recognition of the individual as a whole—mind, body, and spirit. It's a reminder that well-being extends beyond the absence of illness, flourishing in the spaces where our psychological, physical, and spiritual needs intersect. Let's explore how integrating alternative therapies such as art, music, and equine therapy can enrich our mental health care, emphasizing the importance of community, connection, and evidence-based practices in suicide prevention.

Integrating Alternative Therapies

The tapestry of alternative therapies offers a rich palette from which individuals can choose, tailoring their healing journey to their unique preferences and needs. Let's consider a few:

- **Art Therapy**: Moving beyond traditional canvases and paintbrushes, art therapy invites individuals to express themselves through the creative process, tapping into deep emotions in a non-verbal way.
- **Music Therapy**: This therapy uses music's universal language to facilitate emotional expression, reduce anxiety, and strengthen social connections.

- **Equine Therapy**: Interaction with horses offers a unique opportunity for emotional growth and learning. These sensitive animals reflect our emotions and reactions, providing instant feedback.

Each of these therapies expands the scope of mental health care, offering avenues for expression, healing, and connection that traditional talk therapies may not reach.

Whole-Person Care

The cornerstone of holistic mental health care is its emphasis on treating the whole person. This approach recognizes that:

- **Physical Health Influences Mental Health**: Regular physical activity, nutrition, and sleep all play critical roles in our mental well-being.
- **Spiritual Well-being**: For many, spiritual practices and beliefs are integral to their sense of self and resilience. Whether through meditation, prayer, or connection to nature, these practices offer solace and strength.
- **Emotional and Psychological Needs**: Addressing these needs involves more than managing symptoms; it's about nurturing resilience, self-understanding, and growth.

Each aspect of our being is interconnected, influencing and supporting the others. In recognizing this, holistic care offers a more comprehensive and compassionate framework for suicide prevention and mental health care.

Community and Connection

Humans are inherently social beings, and our well-being is deeply tied to our connections with others. Holistic approaches to mental health care emphasize the importance of:

- **Building Supportive Communities**: It is crucial to foster environments where individuals feel understood and supported, whether through support groups, communal activities, or online forums.
- **Strengthening Social Bonds**: Encouraging strong and healthy relationships with family, friends, and peers provides a network of support that can be life-saving for someone struggling with suicidal thoughts.
- **Volunteering and Contribution**: Engaging in activities that contribute to the well-being of others can provide a sense of purpose and belonging, reinforcing one's value within a community.

These connections offer support and remind us of our place within a more extensive web of relationships, providing strength and perspective in challenging times.

Evidence-Based Practices

While the appeal of holistic approaches is clear, their incorporation into mental health care must be guided by evidence of their effectiveness. Research into these therapies has shown promising results:

- Studies on **art therapy** have highlighted its ability to reduce symptoms of depression and anxiety, offering an outlet for expression that can be particularly beneficial for those who struggle to articulate their feelings verbally.
- **Music therapy** has been shown to significantly decrease stress and improve mood, making it a valuable tool in the treatment of mental health conditions.
- **Equine therapy** has demonstrated effectiveness in improving emotional regulation, self-esteem, and interpersonal skills, making it a powerful complement to more traditional therapies.

These findings underscore the value of integrating these therapies into comprehensive care plans, offering individuals a broader spectrum of tools for managing their mental health and preventing suicide.

Exploring holistic mental health approaches combines traditional and alternative therapies, recognizing the diverse nature of healing. By offering a range of paths to well-being, we acknowledge the complexity of each person's journey. This journey towards health is communal, fostered by mutual understanding, compassion, and our shared humanity.

5.5 Advocacy and Policy Change: A Path to Systemic Support

In the complex interplay of progress and policy, clarity in the steps and the path is often elusive. However, within the realm of mental health care and suicide prevention, the call for change reverberates urgently. This call is heard in schools, on social media, and in personal moments of despair. Advocacy emerges as a potent force capable of reshaping mental health support and suicide prevention. It challenges the existing inertia, paving the way for more compassionate and comprehensive care.

The Power of Advocacy

At its core, advocacy in mental health and suicide prevention endeavors to shift perceptions, alter policies, and allocate resources toward creating a society where support is accessible and understanding is abundant. It's a rallying cry for those whose voices have been dulled by stigma, a beacon for those navigating the darkness of mental illness, and a bridge connecting the lived experience of individuals with the legislative mechanisms of change. Advocacy operates on multiple fronts:

- **Public Awareness**: Elevating the conversation about mental health and suicide prevention to the public sphere, breaking down barriers of misunderstanding and stigma.
- **Policy Influence**: Engaging with policymakers to underline the critical need for improved mental health services and suicide prevention strategies.
- **Resource Allocation**: Pushing for the necessary funding to support mental health programs, research, and access to care for all individuals.

Key Policy Areas

The landscape of mental health care and suicide prevention is vast, yet several key policy areas emerge as pivotal battlegrounds for advocacy efforts. These include:

- **Mental Health Care Funding**: Advocates tirelessly work to secure increased funding for mental health services,

ensuring that care is available and affordable for all individuals.
- **Professional Training**: Highlighting the need for enhanced training for mental health professionals, educators, and first responders, equipping them with the tools to support individuals in crisis effectively.
- **Public Education Campaigns**: Championing initiatives that educate the public on mental health issues, early intervention's importance, and support services' availability.

Engaging with Policymakers

The bridge between advocacy and policy change is built through deliberate, strategic engagement with policymakers. This involves presenting problems and offering solutions backed by research, personal stories, and a clear vision for a better future. Effective strategies include:

- **Building Relationships**: Establishing ongoing dialogues with policymakers, becoming a trusted source of information and insight on mental health and suicide prevention issues.
- **Presenting Compelling Evidence**: Leveraging data, research findings, and personal narratives to underscore the urgency of policy changes and the potential impact of proposed measures.
- **Collaborative Efforts**: Joining forces with other advocacy groups, mental health organizations, and stakeholders to amplify the call for change, creating a chorus too loud to ignore.

Success Stories

Victories, both large and small, mark the path of advocacy, each contributing to the momentum toward a future where mental health is prioritized, and suicide prevention is woven into the fabric of our society. Notable successes include:

- **Legislative Wins**: Advocacy efforts brought the issue to the forefront of legislative agendas and helped pass laws requiring suicide prevention training for school staff in several states.
- **Funding Increases**: Persistent advocacy and campaigning result directly in significant boosts in funding for mental health services and suicide prevention programs at both state and national levels."
- **Awareness Campaigns**: The launch of nationwide public education campaigns focused on mental health awareness and suicide prevention, supported by partnerships between advocacy groups and government agencies, leading to increased public understanding and de-stigmatization of mental health issues.

In every discussion held, policy shaped, and resource assigned, the profound influence of advocacy in mental health care and suicide prevention is evident. It highlights the strength of collective efforts, the unwavering resolve of advocates, and the transformative potential within each individual. By persisting in challenging misconceptions and advocating for crucial policy shifts, advocates pave the way for a society where mental health is destigmatized, and aid is easily accessible. Through advocacy, we envision and construct a brighter future, advancing one policy change at a time toward a more supportive and understanding society.

5.6 How to Start a Conversation About Suicide Prevention

Discussing suicide prevention can be daunting, like being on the brink of a vast chasm, aware of the critical need to move forward but burdened by the uncertainty of what lies ahead. Starting these conversations demands a delicate balance of sensitivity, bravery, and a deep-seated respect for our collective humanity.

Breaking the Ice

Initiating a dialogue on such a sensitive topic necessitates a thoughtful approach that respects the individual's space and readiness to engage. Strategies here include:

- Starting with general wellness inquiries can open the door gently, allowing the person to steer the conversation toward deeper issues at their own pace.
- Mentioning observed changes in behavior or mood as an expression of concern rather than judgment paves the way for an open conversation.
- Sharing information or stories about mental health and suicide prevention in a non-confrontational manner can spark dialogue, offering an external focal point for the conversation.

When navigating these conversations in different settings, tailor your approach to fit the context:

- **In families**, it might start with a shared moment of quiet reflection, an invitation to talk when ready.
- **Schools** can integrate discussions within the health and well-being programs framework, making it part of the standard curriculum.

- **Workplaces** might introduce the topic during meetings that discuss health and safety, prioritizing mental health.

Creating a Safe Environment

The setting in which discussions about suicide take place dramatically influences how they unfold. A supportive, non-judgmental atmosphere fosters openness and trust. Key elements of such an environment are:

- Physical spaces that offer privacy and a sense of security, free from the risk of unwanted interruptions or eavesdropping.
- A clear assurance that the conversation is confidential, reinforcing the sanctity of shared information.
- An atmosphere of empathy and patience, where the pace of the conversation is guided by the comfort level of the person sharing.

Listening and Validating

Active listening is the cornerstone of effective communication about suicide prevention. It involves:

- Giving undivided attention, acknowledging that the moment and the person's feelings are paramount.
- Reflecting back on what has been said to show understanding and to clarify without inserting personal biases or judgments.
- Validating their feelings, affirming that feeling overwhelmed, scared, or alone is okay and that seeking help is a sign of strength, not weakness.

This approach fosters a connection that transcends mere words, signaling a genuine commitment to understanding and support.

Offering Support and Resources

The culmination of initiating a conversation about suicide prevention lies in bridging the gap between discussion and action. Offering support means:

- Providing information about local and online resources, including hotlines, counseling services, and support groups, equipping the individual with tools to seek further help.
- Discussing potential next steps they could take, whether setting up an appointment with a mental health professional or exploring therapeutic activities, and offering to assist in these processes if desired.
- Reassuring them of your continued support, emphasizing that they don't have to navigate their feelings or the path to getting help alone.

It's essential to understand the boundaries of our roles in these discussions, providing support and resources while recognizing when professional assistance is required. Engaging in talks about suicide prevention helps shape a culture that values mental health. These dialogues, characterized by empathy, respect, and a joint effort to comprehend, hold the potential for profound change. They can alter perspectives, break down barriers, and, most importantly, provide hope—a reminder that no one needs to battle their darkest moments solo.

5.7 Creating a Suicide Prevention Plan: A Guide for Families

Families frequently operate as a support network, offering a foundation that each member can rely on in challenging times. This support system becomes even more vital when the possibility of suicide arises. A thoughtfully constructed suicide prevention plan can act as a lifeline, a structured approach ensuring that every family member knows how to respond effectively to signs of distress. It's about creating a safety net woven from understanding, preparation, and love.

Key Elements of a Prevention Plan

A family's suicide prevention plan should be both a shield and a guide, offering protection through foresight and direction through knowledge. Its structure typically includes:

- **Identification of Warning Signs**: Educate all family members about the signs that might indicate a risk of suicide, such as changes in behavior, mood swings, withdrawal, or explicit expressions of hopelessness.
- **Steps for Intervention**: Outline clear, actionable steps to take if a family member exhibits these warning signs. This might include who to contact first, how to approach the individual compassionately, and what not to say.
- **Emergency Contacts**: Compile a list of essential contacts, including local crisis centers, therapists, and trusted individuals outside the family who can offer support or intervene if needed.

Creating this plan should never be a solitary task. Involvement from all family members ensures diverse perspectives and fosters a collective commitment to each other's well-being.

Family Communication Strategies

Open communication is the thread that ties a family's suicide prevention plan together. It's about building bridges before they're needed, ensuring pathways for dialogue are always open and accessible. Strategies to enhance this communication include:

- **Regular Check-Ins**: Establish a routine of regular, informal check-ins with each other, creating a space where feelings can be shared freely without judgment.
- **Education Sessions**: Hold family meetings dedicated to learning about mental health, utilizing resources like books and articles, or even inviting a professional to discuss suicide prevention.
- **Create a Safe Space**: Make it known that home is a safe haven for all emotions, where talking about mental health is encouraged, not avoided.

These strategies aim to remove the stigma surrounding discussions of mental health, making it as natural as talking about physical well-being.

Involving the Individual at Risk

When fear for a family member's safety arises, involving them in creating and maintaining the prevention plan can empower them and reaffirm their sense of agency. This approach requires sensitivity, ensuring they feel supported, not surveilled. Considerations include:

- **Respect Their Input**: Their insights into what might help in moments of crisis are invaluable. This can include preferences for who they would like to talk to and specific interventions they find helpful or harmful.
- **Empowerment Through Role Assignment**: Assign them a role in the plan's creation and upkeep, reinforcing their importance within the family and as part of the solution.
- **Personalized Support Resources**: Encourage them to identify personal resources, be it friends, hobbies, or places, that provide comfort or distraction during difficult times.

This involvement is a delicate balance between offering support and respecting autonomy, ensuring they know they're not alone in their struggles.

Review and Update

The only constant in life is change, and a family's suicide prevention plan must be flexible enough to accommodate this inevitability. Regular reviews ensure the plan remains relevant and effective, adapting to new circumstances, insights, and resources. This process might include:

- **Scheduled Reviews**: Set regular intervals for reviewing the plan as a family, discussing what works, what doesn't, and any changes in the family dynamic that might necessitate adjustments.
- **Adjustments Post-Crisis**: If a family member experiences a crisis, review the plan afterward to identify what was effective in the response and what could be improved.

- **Stay Informed**: As knowledge about suicide prevention evolves, so too should your plan. Stay informed about new resources, strategies, and support systems that could enhance your approach.

In this ever-shifting landscape of mental health, a family's suicide prevention plan is both a map and a compass, guiding each member through the darkest of times with the light of preparedness, understanding, and steadfast support. It's a testament to the power of unity in the face of adversity, a reminder that together, we can face our deepest fears and emerge with hope and resilience.

5.8 The Importance of Crisis Hotlines: A Lifeline for Many

In times of deep despair, making a connection by reaching out can be a crucial turning point. Crisis hotlines act as beacons of hope, offering comfort, a listening ear, and a connection to someone who cares. These services are essential in suicide prevention, offering immediate, accessible support to those in need.

Role and Function

Crisis hotlines serve as critical first points of contact for individuals experiencing suicidal thoughts or severe emotional distress. Operated 24/7, these hotlines ensure that help is just a phone call away, regardless of the time of day or night. The primary objectives include:

- Offering a safe, anonymous space for individuals to express their feelings and thoughts.
- Providing emotional support and crisis intervention by trained volunteers or professionals.

- Guiding callers towards appropriate long-term help and resources.

This immediate accessibility can be the difference between despair and hope, isolation and connection.

Training for Hotline Volunteers

The effectiveness of crisis hotlines hinges on the compassion, understanding, and skill of those answering the calls. Volunteers undergo rigorous training to prepare them for the wide range of scenarios they may encounter, which include:

- **Active Listening Techniques**: Learning to listen without judgment, providing callers with undivided attention, and acknowledging their feelings and experiences.
- **Risk Assessment Skills**: Identifying signs of imminent risk of suicide and understanding when to escalate the call to emergency intervention.
- **Resource Navigation**: Familiarizing themselves with local and national resources to provide callers with appropriate referrals for further support.

This training ensures that volunteers are equipped to offer emotional support and act decisively when immediate intervention is required.

Success Stories

The impact of crisis hotlines is profound, with countless stories of lives touched and saved through these vital conversations. Some narratives include:

- A young person feeling utterly alone with their thoughts of self-harm, finding solace and strength in the voice of a hotline volunteer, guiding them through the night and into seeking further help.
- An individual grappling with the loss of a loved one to suicide who calls in seeking a glimmer of understanding and finds a pathway to grief counseling and community support groups.
- A Veteran struggling with PTSD who, in a moment of crisis, reaches out to a hotline dedicated to supporting military personnel and discovers a network of support tailored to their experiences.

These stories underscore the hotline's role as a critical lifeline, offering immediate support and connecting individuals to a broader spectrum of care and community.

Promoting Awareness

Despite their proven value, the challenge remains to ensure everyone who needs this support knows it's available. Promoting awareness of crisis hotline services is essential, involving:

- **Community Engagement**: Collaborating with schools, workplaces, and community organizations to disseminate information about hotline services.
- **Social Media Campaigns**: Leveraging the power of social media to reach a wider audience, particularly among younger demographics, who may be more likely to seek help online.
- **Partnerships with Healthcare Providers**: Encouraging doctors, therapists, and other healthcare professionals to

share information about crisis hotlines with patients who may be at risk.

By increasing awareness, we can ensure that more individuals know where to turn in moments of crisis, making the first step towards seeking help that much easier.

5.9 Reducing Access to Means: A Preventative Strategy

In the sphere of suicide prevention, the conversation often gravitates toward the psychological and emotional aspects, crucially important yet only part of a broader picture. A vital, albeit less discussed, strategy in this multifaceted approach is means reduction. This method, grounded in the basic principle of limiting access to common methods of suicide, such as firearms and medication, has demonstrated significant potential in preventing suicide attempts.

Understanding Means Reduction

Means reduction operates on a foundational insight: the impulse to attempt suicide is frequently transient. By restricting immediate access to lethal means during these critical moments, the likelihood of acting on suicidal thoughts decreases substantially. This approach does not suggest removing all potential means of suicide, an impractical goal, but focuses on making access more challenging during moments of crisis.

Strategies for Means Reduction

Implementing means reduction requires thoughtful strategies that respect individual rights while prioritizing safety. Key methods include:

- **Safe Storage**: Encouraging the secure storage of firearms and medications, including gun safes and lockboxes, can significantly mitigate risks. This might mean storing weapons and firearms unloaded with ammunition separately. Medications should be kept in locked cabinets, with only limited quantities accessible.
- **Prescription Management**: Healthcare providers can play a crucial role by prescribing medications in limited quantities, particularly those with a high risk of overdose. This practice, coupled with regular follow-ups, ensures that patients have access to necessary medications while minimizing the risk of accumulation.
- **Community Education**: Raising awareness about the importance of means reduction through community programs can foster a collective commitment to suicide prevention. This includes educating about the risks associated with accessible firearms and medications and providing practical advice on secure storage solutions.

Community and Policy Efforts

The effectiveness of means reduction is amplified through community engagement and supportive policies. Community initiatives can include:

- **Distribution of Safety Devices**: Programs that provide free or subsidized safety devices, such as gun locks and medication safes, make it easier for individuals to implement secure storage practices.
- **Policy Advocacy**: Advocates can push for policies that support means reduction, such as legislation requiring safe storage practices for firearms and limitations on the number of medications dispensed at one time.

These community and policy efforts create an environment where means reduction is not only encouraged but facilitated, making it an integral part of the collective approach to suicide prevention.

Evidence of Effectiveness

The question of means reduction's effectiveness is answered in a body of research that underscores its impact. Studies have shown that:

- **Firearm Storage**: Areas with higher rates of secure firearm storage have lower rates of suicide by firearms. This correlation highlights the direct impact of storage practices on suicide rates.
- **Medication Packaging**: The introduction of blister packaging for medications, which makes it more time-consuming to access large quantities, has been associated with a decrease in overdose attempts.
- **Bridge Barriers**: The installation of barriers on bridges known for being sites of suicide attempts has led to a reduction in such incidents, demonstrating the principle that limiting access to means can prevent suicides.

These examples, supported by data, affirm the critical role of means reduction as part of a comprehensive suicide prevention strategy. It's a reminder that, in the fight against suicide, practical, tangible actions can and do save lives.

5.10 The Future of Suicide Prevention: Trends and Innovations

The field of suicide prevention is evolving rapidly, with new technologies and innovative approaches offering promising avenues for saving lives. As we look toward the future, it's clear that integrating cutting-edge technologies, tailored programs for diverse populations, and global cooperation will play pivotal roles in shaping the suicide prevention landscape.

Emerging Technologies

The digital age has ushered in a wave of technological advancements that hold significant potential for suicide prevention. Artificial Intelligence (AI) and machine learning are at the forefront, offering tools that can predict and intervene in crises with unprecedented precision. For instance:

- **Predictive Analytics**: AI algorithms can analyze vast amounts of data from social media posts, search history, and digital communication to identify patterns indicative of suicidal thoughts or behaviors. These insights allow for timely interventions.
- **Virtual Support**: AI-powered chatbots provide immediate, 24/7 emotional support and crisis intervention. These virtual assistants guide individuals to helpful resources and human support networks.

The promise of these technologies lies in their ability to reach individuals in crisis at scale, offering real-time support and bridging gaps in mental health services.

Innovative Intervention Programs

Innovation in suicide prevention also extends to the development of new intervention programs that address the needs of diverse populations. Examples of these pioneering initiatives include:

- **Mobile Health Applications**: Apps that offer self-help tools, mood tracking, and connections to support networks are becoming increasingly sophisticated. They serve as accessible resources for individuals seeking help discreetly.
- **School-Based Digital Platforms**: Educational institutions are adopting digital platforms that facilitate anonymous reporting of concerns, allowing students to seek help for themselves or peers without fear of stigma.

These programs exemplify how innovation can enhance traditional support systems, making suicide prevention more accessible and effective.

Focus on Underrepresented Groups

Recognizing the unique challenges faced by underrepresented and vulnerable groups is crucial in the evolution of suicide prevention efforts. Tailored approaches considering cultural, socio-economic, and identity-specific factors are essential for effective support. Efforts in this area include:

- **Culturally Sensitive Programs**: Initiatives that respect and incorporate cultural backgrounds and experiences into suicide prevention strategies are being developed to ensure relevance and effectiveness.
- **Targeted Support for High-Risk Groups**: Programs designed specifically for groups at higher risk, such as LGBTQ+ youth, veterans, or those experiencing homelessness, are expanding, offering specialized resources and support.

These focused efforts are critical in ensuring that suicide prevention strategies are inclusive and address the needs of all individuals.

Global Collaborations

The fight against suicide transcends borders, making global collaboration a key element in advancing prevention efforts. Countries and organizations can learn from each other and amplify their impact by sharing research findings, best practices, and innovations. Notable developments in this area include:

- **International Research Consortia**: Groups that unite researchers worldwide to share data and insights, driving our understanding of suicide and effective prevention strategies.
- **Cross-Border Initiatives**: Programs that operate across countries, leveraging digital platforms to offer support and resources on a global scale, demonstrate the power of international cooperation.

These collaborative efforts not only enhance the reach of suicide prevention initiatives but also foster a sense of global community united in the goal of saving lives.

Looking ahead, the landscape of suicide prevention shines with hope and innovation. Technology integration, targeted programs, inclusivity focus, and global cooperation are forging fresh paths toward a world where suicide prevention is more effective and empathetic. These advancements not only promise life-saving results but also revolutionize our approach to understanding mental health and suicide complexities.

With each stride taken, we're reminded of the interconnection of our endeavors, the potential for breakthroughs that alter lives, and the shared dedication uniting us in suicide prevention work. As we progress and innovate, we hold onto the belief that together, we can shape a future where fewer lives are lost to suicide and more individuals discover the support and hope they need to flourish.

In the spirit of innovation and collaboration, we press on, prepared to meet the challenges and prospects that await in our ongoing journey of suicide prevention.

Conclusion

As we wrap up this journey through the pages of this book, I'd like to pause and reflect on the path we've traveled together. From exploring the spectrum of suicidal thoughts to fostering resilience and drawing strength from community support, we've delved into the multifaceted world of suicide prevention and mental health awareness. This book has not only touched on the darkness of suicidal ideation but has also shed light on the hope and resilience that can follow.

Our key takeaways highlight the importance of early intervention, community support's power, and mental health education's role. We've emphasized the need to nurture hope and resilience within ourselves and our loved ones, stressing the value of holistic and personalized approaches to mental health care and suicide prevention.

As someone dedicated to my roles as a husband, father, and serviceman, my contribution to suicide prevention and mental health awareness is deeply personal and professional. My aim, shaped by experiences in military and civilian healthcare settings, has been to empower individuals and communities to recognize their strengths, build resilience, and find hope even during tough times.

The insights and strategies shared in this book are universally relevant, offering guidance not only to those directly impacted by suicide but also to mental health professionals, educators, parents, and anyone interested in promoting understanding and support around mental health.

I encourage you, as readers, to take proactive steps in addressing mental health challenges and suicide prevention in your lives and communities. Let this book be a starting point for meaningful conversations, support, and advocacy for positive change in mental health approaches.

The road to mental health resilience and suicide prevention is unique for each person and is marked by challenges and growth. I recognize the trials you may face and want to remind you that seeking help is a brave choice, reflecting strength, not weakness. You're not alone in this journey.

In conclusion, I offer words of encouragement and solidarity. Even amidst the darkest moments, remember there is always light to be found. Hold onto hope, seek support, and believe in the potential of a brighter tomorrow despite whatever challenges might be surrounding you today. Together, we can navigate mental health challenges and bolster a more resilient community for ourselves and future generations.

Below is a list of national hotlines, websites, and support groups for Veterans, individuals grappling with mental health issues, or anyone needing immediate assistance or resources. These resources are available to you and offer support whenever you reach out.

Let's continue learning, engaging in open discussions about mental health, and supporting each other on the path toward healing and resilience. You got this! We got this! Together we are strong!

With heartfelt solidarity,

Vernon Mullins

THE ESSENTIAL GUIDE TO SUICIDE PREVENTION

Transformative Strategies for Reducing Self-Harm, Enhancing Mental Health, and Building Personal Resilience

Now that you have the tools to help prevent suicide and build inner strength, it's time to share your new knowledge. By doing so, you can guide others to find the same hope and support you have discovered.

By leaving your honest thoughts about this book on Amazon, you'll show others—people just like you—where they can find the help they're looking for. You'll pass on the light of understanding and compassion.

Thank you for your kindness. The journey of healing and resilience grows when we share what we've learned. You're helping me keep this important conversation alive.

Utilize the following link or scan the QR code below to leave your review on Amazon:

https://www.amazon.com/review/review-your-purchases/?asin=B0DH9TZ2C9

With hope & sincerity,

Vernon Mullins, MSN, APRN, FNP-BC

Quick Access Reference List for Suicide Prevention and Awareness

1. National Suicide Prevention Lifeline (U.S.)

- Phone: 1-800-273-TALK (1-800-273-8255)
- Website: suicidepreventionlifeline.org

2. Crisis Text Line

- Text: HELLO to 741741
- Website: crisistextline.org

3. Veterans Crisis Line

- Phone: 1-800-273-8255, Press 1
- Text: 838255
- Website: veteranscrisisline.net

4. Substance Abuse and Mental Health Services Administration's National Helpline

- Phone: 1-800-662-HELP (1-800-662-4357)
- Website: samhsa.gov/find-help/national-helpline

5. National Alliance on Mental Illness HelpLine

- Phone: 1-800-950-NAMI (1-800-950-6264)
- Website: nami.org/help

6. Lifeline for LGBTQ+ Youth (The Trevor Project)

- Phone: 1-866-488-7386
- Text: START to 678678
- Website: thetrevorproject.org

7. Trans Lifeline

- Phone: (US) 877-565-8860, (Canada) 877-330-6366
- Website: translifeline.org

8. Teen Line

- Phone: 1-800-852-8336
- Text: TEEN to 839863
- Website: teenlineonline.org

9. Disaster Distress Helpline

- Phone: 1-800-985-5990
- Text: TalkWithUs to 66746
- Website: disasterdistress.samhsa.gov

10. Boys Town National Hotline

- Phone: 1-800-448-3000
- Text: VOICE to 20121
- Website: boystown.org

11. Young Women's Christian Association USA

- Website: ywca.org

12. American Foundation for Suicide Prevention

- Website: afsp.org

13. Rape, Abuse & Incest National Network

- Phone: 1-800-656-HOPE (1-800-656-4673)
- Website: rainn.org

14. HopeLine Network

- Website: hopeline.com

15. Mental Health America

- Website: mhanational.org

16. The Jed Foundation

- Website: jedfoundation.org

17. Project Semicolon

- Website: projectsemicolon.com

18. Active Minds

- Website: activeminds.org

19. To Write Love on Her Arms

- Website: twloha.com

20. Substance Abuse and Mental Health Services Administration

- Website: samhsa.gov

These resources offer support for individuals facing suicide, mental health crises, or emotional challenges and are available to assist individuals, families, and Veterans round the clock!

References

- 10 fundraising ideas for mental health nonprofits. (2024). *Qgiv.* https://www.qgiv.com/blog/fundraising-ideas-mental-health-nonprofits/
- 10 grief counseling therapy techniques & interventions. (2018, April 25). *Positive Psychology.* https://positivepsychology.com/grief-counseling/
- A beginner's guide to setting SMART goals in recovery. (2024). *October Road Inc.* https://www.octoberroadinc.net/a-beginners-guide-to-setting-smart-goals-in-recovery/
- A comprehensive approach to suicide prevention. (2020, September). *Suicide Prevention Resource Center.* https://sprc.org/effective-prevention/comprehensive-approach
- Bahk, Y. C., Jang, S. K., Choi, K. H., & Lee, S. H. (2017). The relationship between childhood trauma and suicidal ideation: Role of maltreatment and potential mediators. *Psychiatry Investigation, 14*(1), 37–43. https://doi.org/10.4306/pi.2017.14.1.37
- Blog, S. (2023, September 18). Study reveals most effective school-based suicide prevention programs - Research horizons. *Research Horizons.* https://scienceblog.cincinnatichildrens.org/study-reveals-most-effective-school-based-suicide-prevention-programs/
- Bondar, J., Babich Morrow, C., Gueorguieva, R., Brown, M., Hawrilenko, M., Krystal, J. H., Corlett, P. R., & Chekroud, A. M. (2022). Clinical and financial outcomes associated with a workplace mental health program before and during the COVID-19 pandemic. *JAMA Network Open, 5*(6), e2216349. https://doi.org/10.1001/jamanetworkopen.2022.16349
- Caring for your mental health. (2024, February). *National Institute of Mental Health (NIMH).* https://www.nimh.nih.gov/health/topics/caring-for-your-mental-health
- Clinic, C. (2024, April 30). Why volunteering can benefit your mental health. *Cleveland Clinic.* https://newsroom.clevelandclinic.org/2022/11/28/why-volunteering-can-benefit-your-mental-health
- Community-based approaches to suicide prevention: New resources and future directions | National Action Alliance for Suicide Prevention. (2017, April 12). https://theactionalliance.org/events/community-based-approaches-suicide-prevention-new-resources-and-future-directions

- Community connectedness for suicide prevention - RHIhub toolkit. (2024). *Design Patterns for Mental Health.* https://designpatternsformentalhealth.org/principles/create-a-safe-space/
- Crego, A., Yela, J. R., Riesco-Matías, P., Gómez-Martínez, M. Á., & Vicente-Arruebarrena, A. (2022). The benefits of self-compassion in mental health professionals: A systematic review of empirical research. *Psychology Research and Behavior Management, 15,* 2599–2620. https://doi.org/10.2147/PRBM.S359382
- de Aguiar, K. R., Bilhalva, J. B., Cabelleira, M. D., Guimarães, G. O., Madureira, T., Agako, A., de Souza, M. S., & Souza, L. D. M. (2022). The impact of mindfulness on suicidal behavior: A systematic review. *Trends in Psychiatry and Psychotherapy, 44,* e20210316. https://doi.org/10.47626/2237-6089-2021-0316
- DuBois, R. (2020). Integrating technology into mental healthcare. *Psychotherapy.net.* https://www.psychotherapy.net/article/integrating-technology
- Effectiveness of complementary and integrative medicine on patients with suicidal ideation. (n.d.). *PMC.* https://www.ncbi.nlm.nih.gov/pmc/articles/PMC8035924/
- Empathy is the missing piece to suicide prevention. (n.d.). *U.S. Naval Institute.* https://www.usni.org/magazines/proceedings/2022/august/empathy-missing-piece-suicide-prevention
- Feeling suicidal. (2024). *Beyond Blue.* https://www.beyondblue.org.au/mental-health/feeling-suicidal
- For community and faith leaders. (2024). *SAMHSA.* https://www.samhsa.gov/mental-health/how-to-talk/community-and-faith-leaders
- Fortuna, K. L., Solomon, P., & Rivera, J. (2022). An update of peer support/peer provided services underlying processes, benefits, and critical ingredients. *Psychiatric Quarterly, 93*(2), 571–586. https://doi.org/10.1007/s11126-022-09971-w
- Garnett, M. F., Spencer, M. R., & Weeks, J. D. (2023). Suicide among adults ages 55 and older, 2021. https://doi.org/10.15620/cdc:133701
- Helping people, changing lives: 3 health benefits of volunteering. (n.d.). *Mayo Clinic Health System.* https://www.mayoclinichealthsystem.org/hometown-health/speaking-of-health/3-health-benefits-of-volunteering#:~:text=Volunteering%20reduces,memory%20in%20adults
- Hou, X., Wang, J., Guo, J., Zhang, X., Liu, J., Qi, L., & Zhou, L. (2022). Methods and efficacy of social support interventions in preventing suicide: A systematic review and meta-analysis. *Evidence-Based Mental Health, 25*(1), 29–35. https://doi.org/10.1136/ebmental-2021-300318

- Kirchner, S., & Niederkrotenthaler, T. (2024). Experiences of suicide survivors of sharing their stories about suicidality and overcoming a crisis in media and public talks: A qualitative study. *BMC Public Health, 24*(1). https://doi.org/10.1186/s12889-024-17661-4
- Luoma, J. B., & Villatte, J. L. (2012). Mindfulness in the treatment of suicidal individuals. *Cognitive and Behavioral Practice, 19*(2), 265–276. https://doi.org/10.1016/j.cbpra.2010.12.003
- Mehl-Madrona, L., & Mainguy, B. (2014). Introducing healing circles and talking circles into primary care. *The Permanente Journal, 18*(2), 4–9. https://doi.org/10.7812/TPP/13-104
- Melia, R., Francis, K., Hickey, E., Bogue, J., Duggan, J., O'Sullivan, M., & Young, K. (2020). Mobile health technology interventions for suicide prevention: Systematic review. *JMIR mHealth and uHealth, 8*(1), e12516. https://doi.org/10.2196/12516
- Pennock, S. F. (2024, July 26). Resilience in positive psychology: How to bounce back. *PositivePsychology.com.* https://positivepsychology.com/resilience-in-positive-psychology/
- Preventing suicide in schools—A systemwide approach. (2022, May 27). *EDC.* https://www.edc.org/blog/preventing-suicide-schools-systemwide-approach
- Preventing suicide: A resource for media professionals. (n.d.). *World Health Organization.* https://www.who.int/publications-detail-redirect/9789240076846
- Preventing suicide: A toolkit for high schools. (2024). *Youth.gov.* https://youth.gov/feature-article/preventing-suicide-toolkit-high-schools
- Renemane, L., Kivite-Urtane, A., & Rancans, E. (2021). Suicidality and its relation with physical and mental conditions: Results from a cross-sectional study of the nationwide primary care population sample in Latvia. *Medicina (Kaunas, Lithuania), 57*(9), 970. https://doi.org/10.3390/medicina57090970
- Selby. (2023, August 7). Building resilience and emotional intelligence: Social-emotional learning activities for high school students. *Everyday Speech.* https://everydayspeech.com/sel-implementation/building-resilience-and-emotional-intelligence-social-emotional-learning-activities-for-high-school-students/
- Silverman, M. N., & Deuster, P. A. (2014). Biological mechanisms underlying the role of physical fitness in health and resilience. *Interface Focus, 4,* 20140040. https://doi.org/10.1098/rsfs.2014.0040
- Swaim, E. (2022, May 28). How telling your story in narrative therapy may help heal trauma. *Healthline.* https://www.healthline.com/health/

mental-health/narrative-therapy-for-trauma
- Thomas, S. (2023, September 6). Life after trauma: It takes a community - Healing. *Insight Digital Magazine.* https://www.thechicagoschool.edu/insight/from-the-magazine/life-trauma-takes-community/
- U of U Health Authors & Marketing and Communication. (2023, January 20). The impact of social media on teens' mental health. *University of Utah Health.* https://healthcare.utah.edu/healthfeed/2023/01/impact-of-social-media-teens-mental-health
- VA.gov | Veterans Affairs. (2024). https://www.mentalhealth.va.gov/suicide_prevention/
- VA.gov | Veterans Affairs. (2024). https://www.ptsd.va.gov/professional/treat/cooccurring/suicide_ptsd.asp
- VDOE Staff. (2022). Suicide prevention. *Virginia Department of Education.* https://www.doe.virginia.gov/programs-services/student-services/prevention-strategies-programs/suicide-prevention-resources
- Wellpoint Care Network. (2023, June 5). Art therapy proven to be successful alternative to traditional talk therapy. *Wellpoint Care Network.* https://wellpointcare.org/media-and-events/blog-stories/art-therapy-proven-to-be-successful-alternative-to-traditional-talk-therapy
- White-Gibson, Z. (2022, May 19). How can art therapy help with trauma? *Psych Central.* https://psychcentral.com/ptsd/art-therapy-for-trauma
- World Health Organization. (2024, August 29). Suicide. https://www.who.int/news-room/fact-sheets/detail/suicide
- Young, I. T., Iglewicz, A., Glorioso, D., Lanouette, N., Seay, K., Ilapakurti, M., & Zisook, S. (2012). Suicide bereavement and complicated grief. *Dialogues in Clinical Neuroscience, 14*(2), 177–186. https://doi.org/10.31887/dcns.2012.14.2/iyoung

www.ingramcontent.com/pod-product-compliance
Lightning Source LLC
Chambersburg PA
CBHW050734010526
44107CB00010B/846